To the three most important women in
inspired me to achieve and excel in an
genuinely set my heart and mind to. F
selflessness and sacrifice of my angel
the unwavering support of my mom, Sade, and sister, Tessy.

Whilst who we are and the person we've been are, to a vast degree, influenced by the nature of our upbringing, enduring life lessons, environment, social orientation and associations; who we can become will purely be determined by our inner motivations and decisions - Jamal Lanre Shashore

Author's Note

If hope is that pillar upon which our very human existence rests, optimism is the vehicle that drives us towards excelling in all that we do. That said, optimism devoid of the courage to pursue our goals would, in itself, be an exercise in futility.

Can any society really consider itself progressive, or great, if its men and women lack the self-motivation tools, techniques and strategies to overcome the personal obstacles lying between them and the fulfilment of their goals, dreams, aspirations and, ultimately, life's purpose? In times of adversity, with nowhere to turn, it is not uncommon for us to seek solutions from external sources whilst neglecting the most powerful human resource of all at our disposal – our inner strength.

By inner strength I refer to the resilient force resident within which not only instils in us the hope we need to survive when navigating the harshest and most treacherous of life's terrains but, more significantly, the optimism and courage we require to thrive in everything we do, or aspire to.

By sharing my most intimate personal motivational philosophies, thoughts and ideas with you, in the form of these daily inner conversations, it is my belief that the *Self-Motivation Diary of a Born Optimist* can be influential in helping you to challenge the negative thoughts standing between you and the accomplishment of your personal goals and objectives. Similarly, when it comes to overcoming life's seemingly never-ending sequence of obstacles on the road to fulfilling our aspirations, it is my hope that you'll find a worthwhile companion within the pages of these day-to-day thoughts and philosophies.

I see constructive transformation in behaviour as a positive transition in personality – a process through which the quality of thoughts and emotions we generate on a day-to-day basis are consciously (and continuously) developed and enhanced to such an extent that our ability to instantly connect with our inner strength, resources, and capacities for problem-solving in difficult situations ultimately becomes second nature.

Like a blank canvass eagerly awaiting its artist's first paint impressions, open the windows of your mind and embark on this life-enhancing journey with me.

The Born Optimist Self-knowledge Proclamation:

I know who I am, I know what I am capable of, I know what I've been through, and I know what I aspire to.

Day 1

My life's journey is a marathon and not a sprint; a race I intend to win not by being the quickest, but by being the most resilient.

I have woken up to yet another Monday morning, but within me resides an indescribable feeling that assures me that this particular Monday will be like no other I've witnessed, or will ever again experience. Even though my previous Mondays habitually dragged themselves along drowsily through the abyss of time, there is something about this morning which fills me with hope and optimism that a brand new era of personal prosperity has begun.

In the face of life's numerous struggles and the sometimes high-octane nature of its challenges, I accept that any kind of success devoid of the slightest degree of adversity should be avoided. And because of my willingness to endure that adversity which I cannot cure, my feet shall remain firmly planted upon the ground like a timeless rock perched on the rough terrains of time. Armed with an acceptance of yesterday's setbacks, my optimism for a successful future will know no bounds for I will remain unfazed and unmoved in spite of the magnitude of the trials that may confront me.

As long as I constantly remind myself of my own unique calling in life – a calling that probably bears no semblance whatsoever to those of others around me – I know I will be just fine. And because I perceive the word 'pressure' as merely a cue for me to put in my very best performance in every undertaking, rather than a synonym for fear or trepidation, I shall rise over and above every obstacle – physical and psychological – that litters the path leading to inner well-being, personal growth, and the realisation of my full potential. As I am prepared to believe in my own uniqueness as an individual like no other, I will constantly seek to identify, hone, harness and develop my potential by utilising the motivational resources lying untapped both within and around me in order to equip my life with a wide range of success-inducing options. For a life filled with options is one that is better prepared to weather unforeseen storms. Most importantly of all, I will strive each day to use my talents and gifts, not only to better myself, but also for the greater good of humankind.

Whilst acknowledging that I am not without my own unique brand of flaws, limitations and inadequacies, I remain deeply encouraged, for I consider myself privileged to be able to learn from such shortcomings instead of being overwhelmed or consumed by them. As for this day; it will be the first of many that sees me ceasing to entertain self-limiting thoughts and negative emotions.

In respect of the competition; rather than aimless hero-worshipping or developing an inferiority complex, I can simply choose to applaud and celebrate the achievements of others for inspirational and self-motivation purposes. And in my personal lexicon of success, there will be no room for the words 'hate', 'jealousy', 'envy' or 'bitterness'.

Negative emotions aimed towards others will have no place in my life; for I believe that harbouring inner resentment towards my fellow man or woman, and their accomplishments, not only represents an impediment to my own spiritual growth and personal development, it is also counterproductive to my quest for success and achievement. Holding grudges against others is as harmful and futile as consciously treating myself to a plate of delicious, yet poisonous, mushrooms whilst curiously expecting to see the demise of my so called 'adversaries'. And rather than passively allowing toxic thoughts or emotions to corrupt my mind, perhaps a healthier approach would be to proactively channel that same energy, effort and strategy towards improving my own life and the lives of others.

To attain the best possible outcome in all that I do I will seek out both performance and productivity enhancement options that are ideally suited to me and my personal circumstances. On a day-to-day basis, I will aim to self-monitor my thoughts and behaviour; placing special emphasis on understanding how ingrained core beliefs, values and assumptions may have affected me in the past and still continue to impact my current circumstances and, potentially, future outcomes. I will remain open to the possibility that the personal meaning and interpretations I assign to certain situations, circumstances and the events in my life largely determine my eventual outcome. Apart from the quality of relationships I share with others and the world around me in general, the relationship I hold with myself is of paramount significance. And should I find my core beliefs and assumptions about myself and others disabling or interfering with my progress, I will make concerted efforts to review and modify them. Just because those core beliefs and assumptions represent notions and values I inherited, or imbibed from childhood and took through to adulthood, does not necessarily make them right. Even though I am a product of my environment (physical and psychological), orientation, enduring life lessons and experiences, it does not mean that I have to be enslaved by these factors. If I so will it, I am more than capable of rising above any situation I find debilitating to maximise my potential and create new, liberating mental and physical pathways towards a progressive future.

Today affords me the glorious opportunity to be my own person. The paths other men and women have chosen in reaching their respective goals or destinations should never unsettle me, since every contender on the race track of life each has their own unique calling and purpose to fulfil. On this very same race track of life, there will be marathoners and there will be sprinters. Come to think of it, can either category of 'athlete' in this race genuinely lay claim to being superior to the other, considering both are accomplished masters of their chosen event?

My fresh perspective on life has reinforced the salient need to not only create a vision of my unique path in life, but also map out a unique plan of action, timescale and a compelling motivational reason (that holds an emotionally significant meaning to me alone) for the attainment of each and every one of my goals, dreams and aspirations.

I aim to thrive under pressure, by rising above life's negative stress and adversity as I begin to feel an upsurge in my confidence levels. And the higher the surge, the closer I'll find myself being gravitated towards the attainment of my set goals.

Before I retire to sleep tonight, I will use this moment of sweet quietness to reflect on this precious gift of life and existence with which I have been blessed. I will, in the same vein, remain thankful that each new day – be it a Monday or a Friday – presents to me yet another opportunity to be a shining beacon of inspiration and encouragement to others around me.

As for me, being alive probably represents the biggest challenge in life, over and above all other potential challenges. With every breath I take comes new opportunities and limitless possibilities for me to put right the wrongs of yesterday and to build on my achievements for the purpose of attaining greater successes for today and tomorrow. I am, and continue to be, appreciative for being part of the competitive nature of everyday life and, if I had to do it all over again, why do things differently? So long as I'm not deprived of oxygen, then I am still breathing; and if I'm still breathing, then I am most definitely still winning. As for everything else life, in its erratic nature and wisdom, chooses to throw at me, I remain safe in the self-knowledge and self-belief that my inner abilities will not be outnumbered, out-thought or out-fought in overcoming each of my outward adversities.

Day 2

Whilst self-doubt incarcerates and impedes my personal growth and progress, self-belief emancipates me and fuels my drive and desire for success.

I am consciously affirming today as the day that the old slumbering giant within me finally awakens to the fulfilment and realisation of its true potential and life's purpose. A day in which I begin to learn how to accord less stressful meanings and interpretations to what I may initially perceive as distressing situations. A day I've earmarked for imbibing a new set of truths and belief systems which show that negative emotions and rigid thinking leads to self-limiting actions and decisions that, in turn result in undesirable outcomes. I will also open my mind to meanings and interpretations by learning how the nature of a person's subjective appraisal of the circumstances in his or her life by far outweighs the actual impact of the circumstances in question. I will come to understand and embrace this as the most significant determinant factor when it comes to sinking or staying afloat in the crisis situations life sometimes hands out. No longer will I remain a mere passenger in the vehicle of fear – a victim of circumstance who is driven to a destination he has no say in, let alone influence in the direction taken to reach there.

The moment has come for me to make the transition from being the driven to being the driver; a once in a lifetime opportunity to transform myself from fear's helpless passenger into that person who is in the driving seat of the limitless possibilities life has presented to me. From this day onwards I will assume the role of the 'engineer' of my own happiness which, in adverse moments and periods of personal hardships and difficulties, will transport me from mere survival to a position where I can thrive and prosper. And even when I'm faced with, what appears to be, the most precarious of life's conditions I will generate reminders to make me acknowledge that somewhere, somehow, there always exists a 'worse' situation. For every painful memory my 'sadness' aims to revisit, the 'hope' and 'optimism' I harbour within will strive to forget, and for every negative emotion I experience, I will aim to locate at least three positive memories to counteract them.

Even though life is forever erratic, due to its complexities, I can choose a self-assured nature over my worries and constancy of purpose over anxieties. And even though the borders of my mind may not always be successful in repelling the entry of intrusive thoughts and negative images, I am strengthened in the knowledge that, with sustained mental practice, I can work on my self-awareness to spot negative thoughts and emotions; and whilst I accept these feelings and emotions as real, I refuse to see them as logical.

For resilience, I will tap into my reservoir of 'success memories' – the areas of my life in which I have been triumphant when confronted with certain challenges in the past; moments when the walls around me seemed to be caving in and the possibility of victory – albeit initially – seemed as realistic as finding polar bears in the scorching heat of the Sahara desert. Equally, if I am prepared to put in the required effort and practice I can learn to reframe my thought patterns by replacing the negative and destructive ones with positive and constructive alternatives. No matter how unlikely and unattainable some of my set goals may seem, my journey towards their accomplishment will commence one step at a time, beginning from the visualisation in my mind. For the concept of actualisation is meaningless if devoid of, or not preceded by, visualisation. I

7

can also draw confidence in the simple, yet highly effective, approach that by merely making small positive changes in different areas of my life each day I will be, slowly but surely, ridding my life of all manner of personal growth-inhibiting thoughts, behaviours and actions that potentially stand between me and personal prosperity. Gone are the days when I've led a life perennially stuck in reverse gear; for the hour is upon me to bid a final farewell to a life viewed through the rear-view mirror, tainted by fear, lack of purpose and regret over what could have been at the expense of what is or, more significantly, what could still be.

My inner motivation is an offspring of my self-belief and my self-belief will, in turn, give rise to optimal performance and a corresponding desirable outcome in every facet of my human existence – be it career, family life, business, education, projects, finances and social relationships. By embracing past achievements – big and small – and nurturing my inner resources, I will be capable of stemming whatever tide of setbacks and disappointments that come my way.

If I've successfully overcome 'mountains' and defied, the seemingly insurmountable 'rocks' of yesterday to get to where I am today, surely the 'pebbles' of problems that litter my feet today should, in comparison, be of minor concern in the pursuit of excellence. And if I have successfully swam in shark-infested waters in the past and emerged with all of my limbs intact, taking a dip with dolphins today and tomorrow should not, by any stretch of my imagination, be cause for fear or trepidation.

For a brighter tomorrow to be ushered in, I may need to embrace some sense of creativity and innovation. I can also work towards overcoming the disabling duo of deadwood-thinking and stagnation that have the propensity to stop me from tapping into my reservoir of potential. I will strive, brick by brick, day by day, to build for myself a platform that maximises my strengths and capabilities, and resuscitates the repressed gems of talent and creativity which have long lay dormant within me. I will leave my mind open and receptive to fresh ideas whilst constantly reviewing my plans and strategies in response to life's vagaries and unforeseen contingencies.

The concepts of hope, optimism and courage will remain my companions by day and bedfellows by night in all that I think, say or do. For out of what I once saw as a dour, drab and meaningless life, will spring green shoots of recovery and personal prosperity.

Day 3

The road leading to success is a journey that comes in four phases: vision, timescale, plan of action and a motivational reason.

I know that the path leading towards the attainment of my set goals and objectives will sometimes be fraught with setbacks and its own unique challenges. I am also aware that, with a sense of clarity and objective self-exploration, I would soon realise that within me lay vast resources that not only enable me to cope, but prevail. And should I, occasionally, find myself lost and wandering in the wilderness of pessimism, a conscious self-reminder of the dark tunnels I once occupied before spotting rays of daylight will strengthen and encourage me to thrive, and not just survive, those trying times.

For every goal I set myself in life, my understanding of 'what' the goal should be, 'when' I aim to achieve the goal, and 'how' I plan to accomplish that goal are crucial factors in determining how successful I will be in that particular venture. But, inasmuch as the knowledge of all three aforementioned elements is crucial to achieving my set goals, they aren't nearly as significant as my deep understanding of the 'why' behind that particular goal or vision. For not only is my motivational reason responsible for fuelling my passion to succeed, it is the very force that continues to drive me; goading me on assuredly even when my flesh and bones become weary due to the weight of the task that lies ahead. For it is the genuine motivational reason behind each of the things I do, or aim to achieve, that will help me transform what was merely a ray of hope for my desired expectations into concrete optimism.

Today represents the first of many days where the negative feelings and thought processes that have previously held me back from realising my goals, dreams and aspirations are blotted from my mind and confined to the waste bin of oblivion. A day the harmful notions of procrastination and indecision will be swept away – for when it comes to the successful execution of my plans, the thoughts and feelings generated within me as a person will, more often than not, be commensurate with eventual outcomes. Through deliberate and regular practice, I can work towards bringing my day-to-day actions more in line with the positive inner workings of my mind, whilst positive visualisation will become the bedrock of my future success and personal achievements.

The new positive image I generate will serve as a beacon of light to pierce through the dark clouds of uncertainty – and, like a revolutionary sea of change, these images will wash away every remnant of fear, anxiety and apprehension I have perpetually harboured within me with regards to my future aspirations. Visualisation and projections of future accomplishments will be my source of hope to me in my hour of need – the fuel that drives my engine during trying times when I find myself drained and running on empty. These images will be my comforter in my darkest hour, and my springboard when scaling the, seemingly insurmountable, barricades placed between me and personal success; regardless of whether the impediments in question are psychological or physical.

And whilst I feel blessed to have a vision, I remain mindful of the fact that the concept of visualisation, albeit necessary in the realisation of my goals, is, on its own, insufficient. For I know that any goal or visualisation process devoid of an accompanying plan of action, timescale and a genuine motivational reason for its execution would be an exercise in futility.

To this end, I will rise up from my couch of complacency and dedicate my entire being to a more constructive set of ground rules for living with a view to transforming what was merely a mental aspiration to succeed to its physical manifestation. In addition, I will constantly work towards building both the inner motivation and courage to endure short-term setbacks in order to achieve long-term successes. I can embrace the art of practising realistic process goals which are not only task-driven but also involve a moment by moment awareness of each phase of performance leading to the realisation of my desired objective. The goals I set myself will be specific and realistic; the type of goal I will not only find challenging in its implementation, but also time-bound, intrinsically measurable and in congruence with my core values.

As another day on my journey towards self-actualisation draws to its inevitable end, let me bid a final goodbye to, what was once, a life of complacency, procrastination and inaction with the firm conviction that when my now sleepy eyes open again, they will bear witness to my lips uttering the word 'hello' to a brand new world of innovative thinking and action.

Day 4

I shall not tread on the path of prosperity wearing boots designed for mediocrity.

In the face of every adversity, actual or perceived, that lies in wait, I will aim to maintain focus and inner equilibrium regardless of the testing conditions around me. Because I believe that each of my circumstances and outcomes will, to a high degree, be determined by the **mental interpretation** I assign to the challenges in question, I will learn to seek a likely positive interpretation to adverse situations prior to reaching premature conclusions or expecting the worst.

And whilst I am aware of the presence of intrusive thoughts, negative emotions and images that sometimes slip under the radar of my mind's defences when things don't go according to plan, I will endeavour to desist from equating such feelings with rational thinking. It is pertinent for me to understand how my thoughts are driven by my feelings whilst my emotions, in turn, drive my thoughts. Consequently, the more I associate negative thoughts and feelings to what I perceive as distressful situations, the higher the likelihood of me being incapacitated with negative stress. By unwittingly exacerbating the negative effects of the problems around me, I am sustaining their existence rather than ridding my life of their baleful influences.

Furthermore, if my main mission in life is to achieve more positive outcomes than setbacks then it is more than likely that mission may come to fruition if I work on adopting new positive and constructive ways of viewing adverse situations and stress-inducing conditions. Perhaps learning to view adverse conditions and stressful situations as merely transitory phases, rather than permanent states, would be the first step in the right direction. For each time I view my problems and challenges – regardless of their magnitude – as 'phases' rather than 'permanent states', I automatically begin to think laterally not parochially, and proactively rather than restrictively.

I can also learn to understand that a phase-minded approach to viewing any problem opens up a world of options and solutions to me rather than merely compounding the situation in question. For it is only when I exude courage and regard hardships and difficulties as mere 'pit stops', rather than 'final destinations', that I begin to attract hope and optimism signalling the end of what has, for me, been a long and winding dark tunnel.

The world of 'permanent states', on the other hand, is an embodiment of infinite despair and insecurity, both of which make me S.A.D. – stressed, anxious and despondent. And even if some of the negatively stressful elements I experience may be more profound and protracted than others, as long as I continue to see them as 'phases' in my life rather than 'permanent states', not only would an end to them be within my sights but also the desired change I long for. Along with a renewed sense of resolve to succeed, comes a renewed intent to lead a life filled with contentment and intrinsic happiness – an inner energy that enables me to thrive in all of my endeavours and pursuits by enduring short-term hardships in anticipation of achieving long-term prosperity.

Furthermore, should I lack any form of external motivation in my quest for personal success, I will religiously nurture the motivation already within me by recalling, reviewing and replicating past triumphs over pain, disappointment and trauma. By using 'success memories' as a launch pad for self-affirmation and self-empowerment, I strengthen the confidence I have in my own abilities to overcome present and future challenges.

No longer will negative experiences represent sources of inner turmoil and torment for me, nor will they confer upon me a label of victimhood; for I aim to rise over and above the self-limiting emotions of fear, self-doubt, and trepidation. And, slowly but surely, this newly-found, prosperity-bound entity within me will wipe out every single trait of premonition in my thoughts, words and actions. For now is the time to trade in my cloak of despondency and despair for one of inner calm, peace and happiness – the emotional state of mind I need to attract positive outcomes and accomplishments in life. And as for my old glad rags of dreariness and disillusionment, they will become a thing of the past, discarded and replaced with the apparel of hope, optimism and courage.

Day 5

In times of setback I was made for 'bounce-back' not 'sit-back'.

Today marks the dawn of a new day in my life and the beginning of yet another golden chapter on my journey towards accomplishing my goals and future aspirations.

As I take positive strides forward in the direction of pastures new and fresh choices, a yearning grows within me to take one final glance in my life's rear-view mirror in reflection and contemplation of my past choices and decisions – good and bad – which I have made and had to live with. For it is the balanced and constructive interpretations I have chosen to accord to past and present events in my life which instils in me a sense of inner belief and the drive to successfully navigate the turbulent tidal waves of life. Through it all, one thing remains unchanged: my inner resolve to remain calm and centred in the midst of life's raging storms that threaten to overwhelm and consume me.

Not only do I presently find myself extremely comfortable in my own skin but also at peace with the errors of yesterday. And rather than growing older with trepidation and viewing my age as a liability each passing year, I aim to embrace my age – with the wisdom and wealth of experience which will come with it – as an asset to me that can also be of benefit to others around me. For the older I get, the more at peace I will learn to become with yesterday's personal setbacks; viewing my achievements to date with pride and poised in anticipation of tomorrow's limitless possibilities. For I know that to fulfil my potential, today and tomorrow, I have to accept certain negative elements from my past, learn the required lessons and move on from them. And, of the million and one things I can learn from past errors, wrong choices and disappointments, the words 'regret' and 'rumination' will cease to be amongst them. Even when the world presents its own unique range of problems and challenges, I will remain safe in the knowledge that, so long as I continue to relax, breathe, reflect, and visualise images of success, I will do just fine. By recognising that a worse place exists than my so-called 'bad place', I stand as good a chance as anyone in overcoming difficult odds in my quest for personal breakthroughs, irrespective of how high the odds are stacked against me.

Today is also the day I start to believe that, resident within me, are star qualities, unique to me and me alone, and as long as an infinite number of stars align the night skies so will there be a limitless quantity of golden opportunities for me to explore. For the moment I find myself in tune with these star qualities, I will be able to develop my potential and positively contribute to the society. And because my inner resources constantly fuel my appetite to achieve greatness and prosperity I find myself immune to living a life solely dependent on the external applause and validation of the outside world in order for me to excel in anything I set my mind to.

Today brings with it a renewed sense of hope, optimism and courage, empowering me to weather the gathering storms simply because the words 'resilience' and 'endurance' have become ingrained in my DNA. Slowly, but surely, with resolute determination and measured steps, I will ascend each rung on the ladder to success, facing trials and tribulations on the way, to reach the highest summit of personal prosperity. Even though safely navigating life's oceans comes with its own unique perils, I firmly believe that I possess both the mental and emotional stamina to warmly welcome such knock-backs; for in my eyes they are simply opportunities to rise rather than an excuse for the disintegration of my goals, dreams, and aspirations. And because I know that my inner drive will begin to expire the very minute I cease to aspire, choosing to become stagnant will never be an option. For my aspirations are not only an embodiment of those things I long for every single day, but those things I continue to live for – that inner force of nature which gets me out of the complacent comfort of my bed each morning.

From this day onwards, regardless of how catastrophic, profound or prolonged the obstacles I encounter may seem, I will embrace them as necessary transitory phases in my personal growth and journey towards personal achievement. For, as long as my working definition of 'setbacks' and 'stumbling blocks' remain that of a 'means to an end' rather than an 'end in itself', there will be no limit to what I can accomplish.

Day 6

The world may be a stage, and I a mere performer, but if I must perform, the world will remember my performance.

What if I choose to rise and bid farewell to complacency and mediocrity for the sole purpose of leaving indelible footprints on the sands of time? What if, without fear or trepidation, I choose to seize this very moment to take centre-stage in making a memorable mark on humankind by leading a life which transcends living for self alone and positively contributing to society?

Although I may be a tiny speck in the grand scheme of things, I will not let that deter me in striving to make a difference in the lives of others. For the path I aim to pursue will be a sharp departure from narcissism and egotism, and one that will inspire others to also aspire for personal greatness. A path that not only seeks to help build, inspire and transform communities, societies and nations, but also one that no longer allows the altruistic light capable of burning so brightly within the human soul to be dimmed or consumed by the darkness of its self-centred counterpart. Regardless of my life's brevity or longevity, I will always aim to give one hundred per cent in all that I do by committing every minute of each day to enhancing the quality of the life I lead and never its quantity. For I believe that, even after I am long gone, the enduring memory the world should hold of me ought to be more about how well I lived and less about how long I lived for. As I begin to free my mind from its toxic web of self-obsession I will slowly and steadily experience a paradigm shift that tunes my consciousness away from its sole preoccupation with 'self' to the genuine needs of others around me. And, provided I stick to the true essence of an

19

adaptive way of thinking, I will no longer put the dire needs of others to the sword in favour of my own material wants; for I aim to make that life-affirming transition from self-obsessed doer to an altruistic giver.

With focus and determination I can become that man who employs his talents and potential in making the world a better place in which to live and, rather than being a mere spectator, I can become the vehicle and driver of positive change. For I now believe that it is my personal hunger for self-reinvention that will put an end to self-limiting thoughts and behaviours such as complacency and procrastination – two of the many barriers to maximising my full potential.

By looking beyond 'self' and my own immediate needs I will be demolishing the numerous obstacles in the way of humankind's progress and prosperity. I can reach out to men and women in communities beyond my borders, both near and remote, regardless of their race, creed, religion, sexual orientation and culture. For I know, that in order for me to become an 'authentic' human being, I will have to banish xenophobia, racism and all other forms of discrimination and embrace all others, regardless of their dialects, accents and ethnicity. For I feel myself gradually transforming into a new species of human; one who sees beauty in diversity, irrespective of cultural difference. And regardless of race, idiosyncrasies and peculiarities I can learn to embrace the notion that all human beings should see themselves as citizens of the same humankind under heaven, first and foremost, prior to pledging any form of allegiance to borders, communities, nations and countries.

And if, in the words of Shakespeare, I choose the 'world' as my very own 'stage' then surely I am but one of many performers accorded a limited time slot to showcase my natural talents to the world. It may also be that the time granted to me to shine my light upon the world represents my life in its entirety, hence the need for me to rise now and show the rest of the world the unique potential and capabilities I have to offer. Setbacks may come and go, but one thing that will never be an option for me is embracing failure as my reality. In terms of my drive and desire to excel in all that I set my mind to there will be no room for capitulating to negative stress and adversity. It goes without saying that refusing to rise to the occasion when called upon will only serve as the perfect cue for the thousands of other 'performers' patiently waiting in the wings to usurp my place.

The time granted for me to deliver is of the essence, hence my desire to give this moment my all as it may very well be my last. Even though the actual number of years I am destined to spend on this earth remains uncertain, one thing I know for sure is that I will not waste another day contemplating the possibility of failure or the consequences of under-performance; for harbouring these notions in themselves may lead to anxiety and performance paralysis. To the contrary, I will play to my strengths, making my areas of excellence my focal points, until my inadequacies gradually diminish during this all important performance.

As motivation and positive cognitive interpretations draw me ever closer to my goals with each passing day, I will continue to learn from the failings of my predecessors – those men and women who came, and saw, but to their misfortunes became the vanquished instead of the victors. Even though I am motivated, with my eyes firmly fixed on the ultimate prize, I must forever remain humble and grounded to avert the same cata-

21

strophic errors of judgment that other mighty men and women fell prey to.

After all is said and done, why should the question of where my spirit or physical remains end up after my demise be a source of anxiety to me if the things I do in the days leading up to that very moment are a source of comfort and happiness to not just me, but other men, women and children whose lives I have impacted when alive? And whilst I know it is right and respectful to mourn the passing of men in the hour of their deaths, celebrating the quality of the life they led as performers on life's stage should be the real virtue. For when it comes to leaving my footprints on the sands of time, the ultimate choice of living a life of contribution will surely take precedence over that of one consumed by self.

Day 7

For every challenging question life throws my way there'll be a resilient spirit lying in wait with a mind prepared to generate brand new answers!

I will begin today with a mental spring cleaning exercise to purge my mind of all manner of intrusive thoughts, images, and self-limiting ideas, driven by fear. To cleanse my mind and achieve more positive and energising outcomes when faced with adversity I can practise replacing negative, stress-inducing thinking styles, attitudes and beliefs with balanced, adaptive and constructive alternatives. And, when faced with problems that threaten to knock me off my stride, I will work towards substituting raw, untamed emotions and reactions with their proactive, problem-solving counterpart – a brand of demeanour that prioritises seeking solutions to problems over folding one's arms and being overwhelmed by the process. As for stale, counterproductive thoughts and statements such as, 'I'm out of my depth' or 'I can't really do this!' – they will be substituted with lateral ones like, 'What steps do I need to take to make this happen?' or 'That strategy did not work for me the last time; what lessons have I learnt to avoid future pitfalls?'

In my quest to fulfil every single one of my aspirations I will not be deterred by the letter of rejection handed to me in any of life's auditions. Rather than viewing such disappointments as cues for descending into further despondency, I will treat them as an opportunity to reflect, recoup and re-emerge. For it will be during these trying times that I seek out new ways to nourish my inner resources each day. A malnourished mind is the breeding ground for stale and antiquated ideas, whilst a healthy one attracts creativity, innovation, optimal performance and productivity – all of which would inevitably help me to realise my goals and desired outcomes.

In order to successfully surf the crest of life's turbulent waves, which threaten to capsize my vessel of dreams, learning to be attuned to my inner resources is of the essence. To achieve continuous growth I need to remain relentless in my focus or I'll slip into the realm of complacency where flawed and deluded thinking are the order of the day. Furthermore, I will strive to avoid that toxic pattern of thinking that subscribes to the erroneous notion that victory will always be mine for the taking, with or without me dedicating my entire being to the cause. I can also learn to appreciate that obstacles will come in different guises; some of which I will overcome easily, and others, due to the profound and protracted nature of their intensity, may take me a while longer to conquer. All in all, I will take each knock one at a time as a test of my character – some sort of lifelong examination I have to sit in order to determine my intrinsic qualities as that breed of human who will not be denied. To become the very best I can be, it is imperative that I keep the windows of my mind open in order to embrace new ideas; for closing these very windows would mean shutting out the endless stream of possibilities and golden opportunities my mind can attract in order for my life to be more purposeful and meaningful.

Should I experience moments when meaningful ideas seem to have deserted me, or don't come quickly enough, I will remain calm in the knowledge that I am merely moving through a transient phase; a phase in which tenacity, fortitude and perseverance will see me through. After all, I know that a delayed reaction in finding a solution to any challenge I am faced with does not necessarily equate to a lack of response; and just because

my success in any undertaking is delayed doesn't necessary
mean that I will forever be denied that very success which I
seek.

Day 8

Adversity presents me with two bold choices: either crumble like a cookie made from flour or to be firmly rooted like a pillar made from concrete.

Today is the day I once again remind myself that the concept of adversity and its consequential impact on my everyday life will continue to be what I want it to be or exactly what I choose to make of it: an unwanted guest paying me a brief visit or a lifetime squatter living under my roof with no intention of ever bidding me farewell! For me, the choice can be clear; I aim to treat each of my life's adversities as nothing more than transitory relationships – in other words, what could be referred to as 'visitors merely passing through'. And should these 'visitors', for reasons best known to them, decide to overstay their welcome, I will remain assured in the knowledge that, provided I maintain a resilient spirit with equanimity and fortitude, I will be parting ways with them sooner rather than later. Learning to adopt this perception of adversity can bolster me both physically and mentally to withstand short-term pain in order to attain long-term gain. And even in my periods of personal disappointment, distress and extreme hardship, within me burns flames of hope, optimism and courage, shining brightly, as if to serve as a reminder that my troubled times are only for a season.

Come what may, I know I can succeed in every area of my life as long as I am willing to believe that lying ahead of me is a purpose waiting to be fulfilled which no one else but me can fulfil – a purpose not only worthy of me enduring life's challenges for but, if need be, even dying for. From winter and spring right through to summer and autumn; from the deluge of

26

rain, snow showers and sleets of despair, I will draw on my inner courage to survive life's vagaries. For the vision I choose to hold for my future promises a ray of sunshine after every dark cloud; and if that isn't worth it, what else could there possibly be?

With each passing day I am gradually beginning to understand how every desired output I crave requires a commensurate input in terms of willpower and effort. And, in order to attain the desired changes in my circumstances, perhaps there has to be a corresponding change in lifestyle. For me to realise a change in lifestyle, it is imperative that I address my style of thought and mentally dispose of the things that don't work whilst retaining those elements that do. I am also willing to learn delayed gratification by seeking less of what is widely perceived and accepted by others to be the 'pleasant' life and more of what I deem to be the 'authentic' and 'meaningful' life within the depths of my very core. And because the word 'adversity' in my self-motivation lexicon is nothing more than an undesirable road leading to a desirable destination, I will try not to be too distraught by it. Although I am under no illusion about the potential negative impact of the storms which brew on the horizon in my quest for success, my positive notions of victory and self-belief, will reassuringly goad me on in the face of every setback.

Today, I subject each one of my thought processes, emotions, decisions, reactions, speech, behaviour and actions to the influence of my life's ultimate purpose and calling. Not only will this day represent the beginning of an era that sees me open-heartedly entertain adversity rather than flee from it; it also ushers in personal and spiritual growth from the ashes of disappointment and despondency.

For I have learnt – and perhaps am still learning – that every single one of life's hardships I have faced (and am still facing!) was placed in my path for a purpose: to be overcome in my quest for success rather than something to be avoided. Adversity, to me, should serve as a welcome development; an integral part of me becoming successful and a constant reminder that, when it comes to genuine success, life seldom offers anyone a 'VIP' pass. Whatever it is I really want from life I have to put the effort in; for it's one thing to visualise what it is I genuinely want out of life, but entirely another to actualise it. Hence, conscientiously pursuing my goals, dreams and aspirations, with passion and tenacity, from this very minute will be all that counts.

Rather than allow myself to capitulate to the inner fears, self-doubts and anxieties that emanate from adverse circumstances, I will employ my inner strengths in countering these negative emotions. When my own thoughts prove to be my nemesis, I will practice using inner motivation building techniques such as retrospection – the art of pausing to recall, relive, review and replicate instances in my life where I have had to overcome certain challenges in order to succeed. Also worth remembering is that I am more than capable of reframing my interpretation of situations from a negative and destructive perspective to taking a more balanced and constructive version of events. Whatever goals or ideas I visualise in my heart and mind, I will strive to actualise with resolute determination, backed by feasible strategies and plans of action. And should adversity come calling again, my niggling fears, anxieties and constant worrying will all become foreign concepts to my personal culture and values; for I now view my premonitions as old habits of yester-

day that have today become surplus to my personal require-
ments.

Day 9

Rather than fold my arms and sit in anticipation of change I can rise from my comfort zone and become both the vehicle and driver of positive change.

Regardless of my background, orientation or the start I had in life I can excel in anything and everything I genuinely put my heart and mind to. And as for my age, I am not perturbed by it because I can learn to believe that the older I am, the more of an asset I can become to myself and others around me in terms of my potential and my overall contribution to humankind. With that in mind, I am also cognisant of the fact that the changes I so desire in life need not occur overnight; nor is there an expectation for it to be a hitch-free process. This renewed sense of hope, optimism and courage will inspire me to approach the change I seek one day at a time. From bite-size chunks through to medium and large scale changes, I will consciously focus on averting the traps of inertia and complacency which are usually synonymous with the phrase 'thus far and no farther'.

Like a skilful sculptor carving out a life-inspiring masterpiece from a lifeless rock I will continue to dedicate my time to reflecting and honing my chosen craft, minute by minute, hour by hour and day by day. I can learn to nurture and fine-tune my talent until its erstwhile crude nature eventually becomes a glorious feast for the human eyes. And like the effect of the sun's rays over the earth's surface I aim to use my craft to not only enhance the quality of my life, but also replenish that of others – shining indiscriminately upon the lives of all people regardless of their background, ethnicity and culture. And just like the sun, that never takes the trivialities of differences into consideration before sending its warm rays down for the benefit of the living, I will constantly seek out various avenues to bring love and happiness to the wider world.

In my pursuit of progressive change I will endeavour to match my core essence and values with the recognition, toleration and appreciation of the ones held by my fellow men and women, even when their values and ideologies are a sharp departure from mine. And if the level of change I anticipate does not materialise itself as promptly as I would expect, I will once again – like in previous days – remind myself that, just because my success in a particular pursuit appears delayed, it does not necessarily equate to it being denied. For as long as I can visualise my life moving away from stagnation, it is but a matter of time before the outcome(s) I tenaciously crave come knocking at my door.

Starting with my next door neighbour in my immediate community, to both national and international levels, the hour has come for me to harness and maximise my potential and the knowledge, power (talent and creativity) and influence I've been blessed with for the sole purpose of contributing my own unique quota to both my immediate community and the world at large.

For I can learn to understand that the knowledge, power, and influence I possess at any point in time should ultimately serve one purpose only: to replenish, rather than diminish, others; anything contrary to this is merely weakness disguised as strength.

To make this change a reality, I have set aside today as the one in which I take the first of many steps forward in what I know

31

will be a lifetime journey. A day I choose to no longer be an onlooker or spectator in the grand scheme of progress, but an innovative participant in the process of waving goodbye to a life riddled with obsolete ideas and self-centredness; a life dedicated to goodwill, innovation and altruism. Today marks the beginning of a new lease of life for me – a life transformed from deadwood thinking and gloom-like living into one of joyous human existence.

Day 10

I have chosen purpose and determination as my vehicles of choice in the attainment of success. For they will transport me from where I am today to the place I aspire to be tomorrow.

Armed with purpose and determination, I aim to seize the initiative today by fully taking charge of my own destiny. I can fulfil my personal calling by abstaining from living my life through the lenses of others whose circumstances may be a world away from mine in terms of personal experiences. Whilst mangoes and melons may both be 'fruits', this does not give anyone the right to class them as identical – and the fact that both begin with the letter 'm' still does not conceal how intrinsically different one is to the other. No longer choosing to lead a reactive life, the moment has come for me to proactively steer my life, containing every known dream I have ever nursed from childhood through to adulthood, to my desired outcomes. For it's in the face of adversity and barricades to success that the concepts of purpose and determination become my weapons of choice in my quest for victory. And should any looming tempest or iceberg rear its ugly head with the destructive intent of capsizing my vessel of dreams, keeping calm and steering safely away from the path of catastrophe will be my priority.

No matter what life's storms presents to me, and regardless of the many stumbling blocks which pose as external threats along the way, I will remain inspired, secure and assured in the knowledge that my sheer will to triumph over any adverse situation will once again prevail.

In times of hardship I will neither give in to fear and pessimism nor bury my head in the sands of inaction. But I will, in a determined and purposeful fashion, learn to confront, head on, whatever climate it is I find myself in; for attempting to avoid my personal adversities – as opposed to standing up to them – would only serve as a short-term fix to a long-term problem. Hence, my need to connect with those 'success memories' of mine which remind me in my darkest hour of disillusionment how I swam with life's 'sharks' and 'crocodiles' and resurfaced unscathed. With these experiences in mind, why would I be incapacitated by fear at the prospect of encountering life's 'serpents' that lie in wait for me on my march towards personal prosperity? If my 'success memories' empower me by enabling me to recall how I safely navigated the worst moments of my life, these setbacks ought not to keep me awake at night considering I've prevailed under more precarious circumstances.

My memories of past personal triumph and achievement in the face of seemingly insurmountable obstacles instils me with the hope, optimism and courage to face the more challenging situations of today and tomorrow; all capable of stretching even the most resilient of human endurance levels. And should I ever find myself sinking in the quicksand of self-doubt, self-limitation or undue self-criticism I will endeavour to clutch at the branch of hope and optimism extended to me by the tree of opportunity.

Today is a brand new day and I am determined to make the most of every phase of my ascendancy to the summit of success, because I genuinely believe there is no limit to where my purpose and determination can take me. For these two vehicles empower me with the necessary foresight to see way beyond today's problem in anticipation of a fruitful tomorrow.

Marching on, I will remain mindful of the quality of the thought processes I generate moment by moment. By learning to subject my mind to rehearsals of success, in anticipation of its material equivalent, I'll be utilising its limitless power as the greatest resource at my disposal to transcend spiritual stagnation and regression. I am also prepared to overcome my inner fears and the subsequent negative stress and anxiety that accompany such toxic thoughts and emotions. As I continue to skilfully navigate my ship of dreams, using purpose and determination as a compass, the sight of that island called 'Success' in the glimmering horizon ahead energises and motivates me. For the sight of this destination remains the strongest indication yet that this long, and often perilous, journey draws to its inevitable end where Success in all her glory awaits me.

Day 11

I am confident in my own ability to overcome every one of my life's hurdles, if and when they arise, not because these hurdles won't be tough in nature but because I know I am of a tougher character.

Let me start this morning by substituting thoughts of failure with mental pictures of the things I aim to achieve, how I aim to achieve them and why these goals, dreams and aspirations are of huge significance to me. I understand that the bulk of my personal frustration and disappointment stems from my perceived gap between the expectations I harbour for my life and its current realities – hence, the wider the distance between the two, the higher the propensity for dissatisfaction with life in general. To counteract these negative feelings, it is imperative that I grow accustomed to a simple, yet highly effective, habit of counting my blessings. By mentally noting those things that have gone well for me, and journalising them on a day-to-day basis, I will be replenishing the inner resources I need to combat a pessimistic outlook. More significantly, being tuned into both the 'mini' and 'mega' achievements of my past and present can help bring to the forefront of my mind the experiences of that man, woman or child somewhere in the world who find themselves in a much more precarious and disadvantageous situation than mine, regardless of how bad I perceive my situation to be. I can also learn to become more cognisant of how far I have come from where I once was to the position I presently occupy in my life. Come to think of it: how can success ever materialise if I find myself dead and buried six feet underneath the earth? Hence, if, at any point in time, I ever perceive a past situation as being better in comparison to where I currently am, the fact that I am alive to even think this thought perhaps should serve as a personal reminder that there are still many opportunities of making it back to that very place I regard as 'The Happy Place'.

So long as I am prepared to believe in the existence and potency of my own inner motivation building exercise through the exploration of, and connection with, my core essence, I will not only survive my life's adversities but most definitely thrive in all I set out to do or achieve. Similarly, if I am willing to seek genuine and personal compelling motivational reasons for success from within me, rather than solely rely on the external brand of motivation from others around me, I will excel in anything and everything I set my mind on accomplishing. And even on those occasions when my goals, dreams, aspirations are seemingly impossible to achieve I will remain undeterred; for as long as I never lose sight of yesterday's conquests, bringing today and tomorrow's goals to fruition will be far from impossible.

Feeling a new stream of endless positive energy flowing unhindered throughout my entire physiology today, I can learn to instil that belief within me that the only areas of human endeavour I cannot excel in are the ones which are of little or no emotional significance to me.

In my quest to maximise my human potential to the fullest I will cower to nothing and no one; for the only formidable adversary worth fearing when it comes to being derailed in the pursuit of my goals, is none other than the very image that stares back at me when I gaze into the mirror.

No matter how high the odds are stacked against me, I will treat each episode of adversity as routine; no more than the springboard I need to launch myself towards – and even beyond – the goals and desired expectations I set myself. With each passing moment I will begin to feel a stratospheric rise in my levels of inner belief and self-motivation. With every step of progress, I will learn to embrace adversity for I see myself becoming increasingly immune, and unperturbed by, the distress and despair synonymous with a life of fruitless pursuits lacking in both meaning and purpose.

I am under no illusion that adversity is, and will always remain, an inevitable feature of my life which will come at me in different guises. Through it all, I will remain unmoved in my conviction that lying on the other side of every transitory or protracted pain I experience is a corresponding happiness, peace of mind and enduring gain. Be it in my personal and social relationships, profession or career choices, finances, health and well-being; or just trying to find my rightful place in the natural order of human existence, my success in the areas which hold a personal meaning to me will continue to know no bounds. And because I have chosen to use my adversities as my source of strength, rather than an alibi for submission, there will be no limit to the things I can, and will, achieve.

Day 12

If life was a beach there would be three kinds of people on it: the spectator who is merely content to bask in the sunshine, applauding or deriding the performance of others; the pretender, who often tries to swim but sinks; and the true contender, whom I aspire to become...the one who successfully surfs the crest of each of life's turbulent waves.

I can become a true contender in life if I apply myself to whatever it is I set my heart and mind on achieving. I can rise from my 'couch of complacency' and make concrete efforts towards improving myself. Whilst striving to enhance my actual strengths I will also identify, nurture and develop my potential strengths with a view to not only achieving self-progression but also making a lasting positive contribution to society. I can make both a conscious and concerted effort to move away from the avaricious realm of self-obsession and material pursuits, and in its stead embrace a meaningful life of self-transcendence and altruism. A life characterised by looking beyond my personal needs alone and genuinely seeking the welfare of others.

Today affords me a new opportunity for change. A day my spectator's hat comes off and is replaced with the spirit of contention and participation in the quest to move humankind forward. For once, in my human existence, my true place in life has never been more crystal clear. I am filled with a level of optimism, sparkling brightly like an undying gem, within every nook and cranny of my soul, reassuringly reminding me that I will no longer be a spectator in the arena of change. And no longer will I allow my obsessive fixation with the performance (or lack of it) of other men and women to result in my own non-performance. For this day, like no other, is one in which the labels of 'spectator' and 'pretender' become foreign to my core essence and values.

Day 13

Why limit myself to the blue skies immediately above when the solar system and beyond is mine to explore. Whatever goal, vision or dream my mind conceives, both my heart and the sweat of my hands will surely achieve!

No matter how arduous the going gets, the inherent need to reach my desired goals – be they short, medium or long-term objectives – will continuously reinvigorate me when weariness kicks in. And so long as I am prepared to move from the virtual realm of mere visualisation of goals to the physical realm of executing my plan of action and strategies, I stand a very good chance of achieving my future aspirations.

Putting psychological barricades such as the occasional self-doubts to one side, there is every possibility that I may also be faced with physical impediments and limitations such as my height, weight, natural speed, physical strength and dexterity (or lack of it) in the pursuit of my dreams. That said, the born optimist within me still reminds me that, provided I keep my 'mental home' in good order, my inner strength and steely resolve can guide me over every psychological and physical barricade on the path to personal prosperity.

Even though I am motivated to believe that the true power of positive expectation cannot be shackled by even the most daunting of physical obstacles, I am under no illusion that a weakened mind can undermine my abilities, regardless of my physical prowess or capabilities.

If I so will it, my mind can assume the attributes of infinite elasticity for its potential to stretch far and beyond the scope of any dimension or physical limitations. And the more positive self-affirmations I feed into the fuel chamber of my mind's engine, by engaging in positive inner conversations, the stronger the likelihood of me achieving the seemingly impossible. For the art of inner motivation can help me transform the things I once perceived as the outright 'unthinkable' into the downright 'do-able'.

With this new era of positive mental attitude, I aim to inject elements of imagination, creativity, fantasy and realistic expectation – in equal measure – into each and every one of my aspirations. For not only will my faith thrive on fantasy, it will be augmented with hard work and ignited by a high degree of pragmatism. Today is the day I put my destiny back in my own hands without leaving it to the whim of that abstract entity that sometimes goes by the name 'fate'.

I can become the sole author of my own achievement script. As long as I remain focused and relentlessly think, eat and breathe this desired vision, its plan of action, timescale and the motivational reason, the desires of my heart will, slowly but surely, gravitate towards me. Today is the day my mind and my body form a powerful alliance which work together night and day, consciously and subconsciously, towards the achieving of one dream; the ultimate experience which will see me transported from the place I currently am in my life to that place I've always aspired to be.

Looking back, I have learnt that the majority of limitations I face in my life are a direct consequence of my mind's own creation, for self-limitation seldom evolves on its own. As long as the 'created' remains subservient to its 'creator' I will never give in to these 'limitations'. Furthermore, if I learn not to limit

42

the capacities of my mind by virtue of hope and optimism, and will myself to pursue that vision with courage, my capacity to achieve my innermost desires in life can be free of every known limitation.

Day 14

The less time I spend peering through the tiny windows of my life's disappointments, the more time there'll be for strutting through its great doors of golden opportunities!

Today marks the start of me adopting a brand new outlook on life in general. If there is one shortcoming I intend to eradicate now, and in the future, it would be my often reluctance to acknowledge and applaud my personal victories. Be that as it may, it is the memories of yesterday's triumphs that would cushion the negative impact of today's setbacks, if and when, they arise.

The new me will aim to find inner strength and fortitude in adversity; no longer will I expend precious time and energy ruminating over past setbacks or trying to change situations or events outside of my sphere of influence and control.

I will, instead, learn to utilise other strategies like making personal adjustments in difficult circumstances or adapting that challenging situation to me. And should that prove to be an uphill task, perhaps removing myself from the growth-inhibiting situation in order to have more clarity, reflect and make better decisions may be the answer. For the ultimate crime to my own progress and personal growth – in my eyes – would be to stand still with my arms folded and do nothing.

My personal resolve in the days, weeks, and years which lay ahead is to wake up with a smile on my face each day, inhaling and savouring the sweet freshness of the early morning air. And whilst I continue to bask and immerse myself in my newly found love for life, I will constantly seek to nurture and develop my inner strength in every way possible, for my mind remains my most potent resource.

From the second I open my eyes at the dawn of each new morning I will fall on my knees to express my immense gratitude to the skies up above; for the thought of me still being able to stand on my two feet despite all the odds against that happening every single day is worthy of my thankfulness.

Looking to the future and beyond, I acknowledge that there will be moments in life when I will find myself between the proverbial 'rock and a hard place'. Not to mention the occasions when I am subjected to the overwhelming effect of life's negative influences and tempestuous pressures. When moments like these do occur, I will take them in my stride with an inner smile whispering the eternal words of the born optimist, "So long as I am not deprived of my breath and the motivation I need to rise each morning, achieving my goals, dreams and aspirations will be but a matter of time." For each day that I find myself blessed with the gift of life and for every priceless minute I bear witness to the wonder of nature in all its splendour, I will continue to draw inner strength and inspiration from negative outcomes, be they actual or perceived.

Day 15

The economic recession might be bold enough to deprive me of my job at any given time but it is definitely not smart enough to prevent me from fulfilling my life's purpose.

Should my source of livelihood ever find itself at the mercy of an economic downturn, I will learn to remain steadfast and upbeat in my resolve to weather the brewing storms of life which lie in wait.

And should my employment, or profession, be marred by poor working conditions, the so-called 'office politics' or lack of job satisfaction on my part I will self-evaluate to test how valid that age-long notion of a 'dead-end occupation' really is. For if my future aspirations remain vivid in my mind's eye and I, on a day-to-day basis, engage in activities such as uplifting thoughts, positive inner conversations and behaviours congruent with the materialisation of these aspirations, the 'unfulfilling' nature of any occupation I'm in, be it perceived or actual, would surely become transient and insignificant. If I strive to identify what my personal calling is in life and remain upbeat about it, the dreary nature of my job would grow exponentially in its insignificance in comparison with the profound rewards of realising my goals, dreams, and aspirations. I can, perhaps, make it a habit to remind myself that, when there is a will to thrive and not just survive, there will always be countless ways to 'bounce-back' even in the face of the most extreme setbacks.

The born optimist within me is of the firm conviction that the more energy I expend on being worried about job insecurities, the more susceptible I will become to performance paralysis and anxieties which will, in itself, result in shoddy work, dismal outputs and, consequently, the job loss I feared in the first instance. For the same born optimist within likens a fear and anxiety-ridden life to a dark cloud that consumes rational thought and judgement – the more I expect negative outcomes, the stronger the likelihood that I will ultimately attract into my life the very things that I dread and aim to avert. And as long as I continue to encourage a pessimistic outlook by choosing fear over a solutions-focused approach to work-related stress, the stronger the likelihood that I will find myself leading a stagnated life rather than a progressive one. Hence, the need to adopt a calm and introspective approach; by tapping into my most valuable resource; the problem-solving capabilities of my mind, I know that I can overcome whatever economic challenges stand between me and personal prosperity.

I see myself as a true contender and performer on the stage of life; one who wields the personal willpower to influence the course my own destiny. But to fulfil my life's purpose it is imperative I learn to accept that it is okay to be flawed sometimes, for my life's story need not be about perfection when progression will do just fine. With this in mind, I am also prepared to accept that harbouring realistic expectations of myself, others and situations in general is the most balanced and constructive way to manage the overall effects of negative stress and adversity in my life. For it is only when I am able to do this successfully that I will be able to explore, identify and enhance my very own signature strengths.

I will also continuously seek to amplify my strengths, with a view to using the art of self-mastery not only to develop myself, but to ultimately benefit others. And, in true altruistic fashion, I can also work towards transforming my natural talents into a product, idea or service that would enhance the lives of my fellow men and women. For I still – and will continue to – believe that the knowledge, power, and influence possessed by me or any individual at any given point in time should serve the sole purpose of replenishing, rather than diminishing, the lives of others, for anything contrary to this is merely a short-coming disguised as strength.

My day job, like most things in life, comes and goes; and no matter the illusion of financial stability it presents at the outset, and no matter its perceived brevity or longevity, it will continue to be what it is in the absence of a true personal calling: a short-term financial solution to a long-term financial challenge.

My talents and creativity, on the other hand, present me with the potential of security, stability and a genuine source of happiness that goes beyond the realm of economic uncertainty or job insecurity brought about by inanimate forces or the conduct of others. This, in other words, represents my attainment of wealth and prosperity through the channeling of my natural talents and abilities towards improving the lives of my fellow men and women.

Day 16

Whenever I'm deflated and despondent I will consult my inner strength and resources to keep me motivated and uplifted.

This morning will see me rise from my seat of inertia to take another courageous step forward in insulating my mind and, consequently, every facet of my life against despondency, despair and disillusionment. Today is the day I understand that being positive is not a state that occurs by accident, but rather by design. It will require a sustained effort and practice on my part to regularly identify with my daily triumphs; for these victories serve as a motivational reminder that I've done it before and can, surely, replicate such successes.

In terms of being (or feeling) my best versus being (or feeling) my worst, I can learn a lot from the art of self-rating. For instance, if I rate my confidence in my abilities to overcome a particular personal struggle at 10 per cent out of a possible 100, the mere fact that I did not rate myself at 0 per cent serves as evidence that there is always a worse place in life than my perceived 'bad place'. I should also understand that the concept of hope is born through recognition of the things I did (and, perhaps, am still doing) to prevent transition from my perceived 'bad place' to an otherwise 'worse place'. And for optimism to gradually build within me I can learn to engage in sustained introspective reflection until I come up with at least one thing I feel needs to happen even if I am at a loss as to how, initially. For until I see a genuine need for a change within me, making any sort of progress would be nothing short of an illusory concept.

As long as I continue to devote my daily existence to finding at least one valid reason to think living is worthwhile, my victory over gloom and perennial pessimism will always be guaranteed. I can learn to embrace adversity as an unavoidable rite of passage towards success in life, rather than something to run from; for I need adversity for my own psychological strengthening and spiritual growth as well as personal advancement. I can abstain from pursuing a life wrapped in cotton wool; for a life devoid of risks (calculated or otherwise) often pans out to be a life devoid of rewards. And whatever drop of sweat that trickles down my forehead in the process will inspire me to strive for more.

In this life that I have chosen to lead there will be no such thing as a destination when it comes to self-improvement and service to others – for each achievement is merely a pit stop leading to yet another pit stop of more successes.

I know that my sole dependence on external sources, albeit sometimes worthwhile, has the propensity to be detrimental after a certain period as others can only dedicate so much of their time and resources to me. With this in mind, I can learn to recognise that the most effective vehicle for positive change is often the kind of motivation that is internally-derived – that which comes from within me – as opposed to that which is externally-imposed. For that brand of motivation which is externally-imposed upon me can be likened to a spark which is here one minute but gone the next, but the one from within me would represent a steady flame with the potential to burn for all of eternity when fuelled with the right motivational reasons.

I see myself as the most potent source of my own drive and motivation; for whatever my mind selectively attends to, repre-

50

sents that which will hold the highest degree of personal meaning and emotional significance in my life. Hence, the likelihood of me successfully pursuing those ventures to the very end will automatically be increased and, in the process, empower me to break down the barricades erected between me and the realisation of my goals.

I know what I aspire to become in life. Within my mind, the chances of attaining those lofty heights remain ever so bright as long as my day-to-day actions are not at odds with the values and commitment levels required to reach those goals I have long envisioned.

The most crucial lesson I've chosen to take away from today's journey is that the most valuable starting point in the attainment of success in any undertaking is the self; anything contrary to this would be no different from attempting to build a monument of epic proportions on pure sand – with the inevitable catastrophic consequences.

Day 17

The starting point of my self-improvement mission is a thoughts-improvement decision.

Regardless of who I think I am, what I do or may have achieved in life, I will, from this very moment, begin my journey from adversity to prosperity within the sanctuary of my mind. For I truly believe that learning to cultivate the habit of reframing my thought patterns, and finding solace and positive lessons even in the most adverse of situations, will improve my state of mind and consequent outcomes. I am also fully aware there will be occasions when the clouds of doom, despair and despondency gather above my head for protracted spells; rendering me too incapacitated to simply wish them away. Burying my head in pleasant activities, likewise, will not bring me the sustained positive emotions I crave because these entirely depend on the personal interpretations I attach to those situations and events that are sources of negative stress. Perhaps the appropriate step to take would be to make a genuine effort to find a meaning in negative circumstances by identifying at least one thing of value that I can take away from such experiences.

Learning to clear my mind of its cobwebs would be a worthwhile endeavour, for I believe that maintaining a positive appraisal of my personal circumstances is integral to experiencing not only successful outcomes but, more importantly, my overall well-being. I can become a subscriber to the notion that I am a product of my own thought process; and as a consequence, the physical world and circumstances which surround me will always be subservient to the whim of my intellectual capacities – hence, the need for me to proactively manage my mind's activities. From my financial habits (money beliefs), nutritional intake (dietary regime) and social habits, to my outward appearance and all aspects of human interaction with my fellow beings, the way I choose to think and nothing else, encompasses all things that are essentially me. In order to flourish, I need to go beyond the realm of merely exuding confidence, to sowing the seeds of faith and self-belief deep within myself – seeds which have the potential to germinate and blossom from mere acorns of fantasies to actual trees of limitless accomplishments. And as for life's predicaments that have the propensity to make me stressed, anxious and despondent; they will no longer, in any shape or form, blemish the happiness, open-mindedness and positive expectations I harbour towards my future aspirations. My newly-adopted thinking channels will all be aimed at building on my personal accomplishments – big or small. Not to mention the capacity to learn from, rather than dwelling upon, my past failings in order to avert future repetitions. On my journey from the corridors of hope to the realm of optimism I can learn to imbibe a personal culture of steely determination to feel in greater control of my thought processes, conduct, behaviour, decisions and, ultimately, my actions. Actions that not only have the propensity to affect my life, but also those of my key relationships – the individuals who form a significant part of my life; from my family and friends, to neighbours and work colleagues. Likewise, transitory relationships, such as those individuals with whom I have irregular or one-off contact. For me to produce the desired results and better outcomes in all that I do, it is imperative that I gain mastery over my mind for its appropriate use requires constant mental practice. A type of mastery which could be no different from learning to swim, riding a bicycle, to driving a car; I may falter in my first few attempts, but armed with constancy of purpose and practice I will surely prevail, regardless of how high the odds are stacked against me. For constantly practising self-mastery will lead to the alignment of the things I aim for with my behavioural patterns and eventual outcomes.

On one final note, whilst I am aware that my mind is not always the easiest of tools to manipulate, I remain self-assured that with self-discipline and a thought process rooted in virtuous values and principles, achieving the desired outcomes on my part will ultimately be a case of 'when' and never 'if'.

Day 18

For my footprints to be immortalised on the sands of time, my feet will keep striding towards a path of authenticity, self-nurture and a life dedicated to contribution.

Of the many things I may be deprived of in life, there is one that if I so will it, can remain untouchable: my unbridled determination to embrace self-authenticity as a personal code for living.

Achieving 'authenticity' for me would mean merging the world of self-nurture with that of altruism. And exhibiting a righteous conduct in my day-to-day living would mean ensuring that, through my deeds and the work of my hands, I aim to continue making a positive impact on the lives of other. My defining legacy to humanity could be giving hope to the hopeless. I can also dedicate my time and resources to being a source of inspiration to others.

I will continually strive to attain the kind of 'authentic' human existence that strikes a balance between self-preservation and altruism; one which holds me personally accountable for the impact of my thoughts, words and deeds on my life and those of other people. It is, no doubt, a worthy cause for the footprints I leave behind to be synonymous with what I have contributed to humankind as against what I took away from it when I make my departure from Mother Earth. Hence, this day will see me trade my self-centred mode of existence for that which sees the welfare of others as paramount; a day when a meaningful life of being intrinsically good, and staying good, replaces the pleasurable life of merely feeling good. Today, the notion of righteousness finally assumes its rightful place in my life as the ultimate moral compass that guides my feet in retreating from the path of fear, uncertainty and darkness and pursues hope, optimism and courage.

And as the wondrous images of this beautiful new era gradually begin to sink in, I resolve to walk through life and its myriad of adversity and challenges with one mind, one dream and one unassailable conviction.

Day 19

I will take ownership of my feelings in relation to the successes I enjoy and the setbacks I have to endure; learning not to attribute my undesirable outcomes to the behaviours and actions of others – the things they do or fail to do.

From this moment on, I will strive to abolish from my mind that fallacious notion of justifying my underperformance, or non-performance, in any undertaking by referencing the underperformance, or non-performance, of others. I will work towards instilling in me the true meaning of taking ownership and responsibility for my own situations rather than apportioning blame to external forces or circumstances outside of my sphere of influence.

From this day forth, I will learn to appreciate the true beauty of human diversity; one so rich that, even though we all co-exist on the same planet and are homogenous in terms of our physiological attributes, we remain distinctly unique creatures. Not only are we unique in terms of our potential, individual goals and the objectives we set ourselves but, more importantly, of the strategies that we employ to attain them. And even though a common pursuit of happiness unites us all we'll often follow different avenues in getting to our individual 'promised lands'. With that in mind, I will retreat into my inner consciousness with the sole aim of exploring, identifying and connecting with my own unique traits, qualities, and core essence. In addition to learning to make decisions on issues and matters that affect my progress and advancement, I will learn to accept sole responsibility for both the process and outcomes associated with those actions and decisions.

Stepping out into a new era of autonomy, self-determination and intellectual enlightenment I will work towards making the things I do well my focal point, rather than being caught up in the negative stress of my perceived shortcomings or those of others. Going forward, these areas that I know I'm good at will be personally defined as my 'actual strengths' and, rather than class the areas that need improvement as 'weaknesses', I will embrace them as 'potential strengths'.

Striving each and every single day to maximise my potentials and lead a meaningful life – a life dedicated to self-nurture and to the rest of humankind in its entirety – should, for me, become an inalienable right and never a privilege.

As yet another day draws to its inevitable end, the born optimist within reminds me that if there was ever a way of living worth turning my back on, it has to be that which constantly absolves itself of its responsibilities by making others culpable for adverse situations that affect me.

Day 20

Should the effort of realising my goals, dreams and aspirations exhaust me, my vision of the rewards to come will adequately compensate me.

Only with my mind's consent can my body truly withstand all manner of hardships to which it is subjected. So long as I am prepared to keep nourishing my mind with positive thoughts, it can, and will, become an impregnable fortress protected from the corrosive influence of pessimism and despair.

Should I find myself at the point of being overwhelmed by hardship, my inbred fortitude and resilience will remain my steadfast companions. And, as I soldier on, one thing, and one thing only, will matter to me: to fix my gaze of hope, optimism and courage upon the bright lights of personal prosperity that shine on the horizon. Whilst these lights depict my future, the clouds of darkness will remain an embodiment of my past. And no matter the magnitude of the challenges that come with my day-to-day survival, I will remain unfazed; for as long as I relentlessly focus on where I aim to be, and less on where I am or was, victory for me would surely be but a matter of time.

With the dawn of this day comes a new mantra: from the minute I set myself a goal – one which is commensurate with my core essence and values with an equally compelling and personally motivated reason to match – the innumerable barricades to success that confront me will be of little or no concern.

As I once again lay down to sleep tonight, I will remind myself that should this journey of a lifetime become a tedious and draining experience, the visualisation of the rewards at the end of that long and winding dark tunnel will more than adequately compensate me.

Day 21

My life is like a cinematic motion picture. Even when my inner 'villains' deflate me to the point of zero I know that I can call on hope, optimism and courage to uplift and elevate me to the heights of 'heroes'.

I firmly believe that resident deep within me are two opposing forces that have guided my affairs since birth. On the one hand is ignorance, an emblem of darkness, whilst on the other, is enlightenment – the divine symbol of light.

Side to side, like the pendulum of an antique wall clock, there continues to be a shift-like motion between these two forces. And dependent on the state of my moral compass – which I also consider to be my conscience – my thoughts, words, actions and behaviour are forever tied to each one of these two forces of good or bad; light or darkness.

Every time I display virtues such as acts of fairness, kindness, honesty, charity, benevolence, dignity and integrity towards my fellow men and women this is, perhaps, a sound indication that the heroes within me have prevailed in battle, but not the war. Likewise, there will come the occasion when I'll find it easier to be obsessively self-centred rather than altruistic, exhibit dishonesty at the expense of transparency, and irascibility instead of patience and tolerance; these are the days when the inner villains from the motion picture of my life will have prevailed over its heroes.

With regards to the emotional diseases of low self-esteem and the tendency to live in constant fear, trepidation and the premonition of not succeeding I can learn to seek out the golden opportunities lying at the very heart of my adversities. And, like a warm ray of sunshine piercing through dark clouds, I can look forward to newly-found inner strength and growth after every disappointment.

Being blessed with the precious gift of life at birth and gently placed in the crib of hope, optimism and courage I know I can survive and thrive under any adverse situation that confronts me. I am a born winner in my own right; a winner whose story has no room for temporary sparks or blind aspirations. Being alive to witness the dawn of each new day fills me with immense courage and positive expectations for my future. The enthusiastic anticipation of what I can become is the platform upon which temporary sparks of hope are transformed into robust flames of optimism, giving me the courage to march on, determinedly, towards successful outcomes.

As a brand new dawn slowly ushers its way into my life I will always remember that I am not alone when dealing with life's challenges. The hitherto snoozing giant within me has now awoken, propped up by courage to take centre stage once again in helping me to fight my battles.

And, as I look heavenwards, I find myself gravitating towards the path to the fulfilment of my purpose – a purpose which is, and will continue to be, an embodiment of self-progression and contribution to society.

Day 22

What some choose to label as 'failure' I have opted to embrace as ' an opportunity turned inside out'.

I can learn to endure both short-term and protracted setbacks in order to attain my long-term goals and objectives. The moment has come to mentally prepare myself for taking on life's tumultuous knocks in order to become the very best person that I can become. A day I become receptive to the idea that attaining success not only requires being open to enduring transitory pain for the purposes of long-term gain, but also a willingness to embrace the bigger picture when faced with difficulties. A day when the born optimist within reinforces the message that to succeed in any undertaking it is imperative I learn the art of finding meaning in every unsavoury event and adverse condition. By adopting the natural inclination to readily perceive unfavourable outcomes in the context of a means to an end rather than being viewed as an end in itself, would perhaps, be the first step in the right direction. For every exaggerated flaw that my mental magnifying glass projects, there exists a mental compound microscope somewhere within me that meticulously adjusts my lenses to spot a corresponding brilliance.

Perhaps, I can also learn to understand that only a mentality rooted in hope, optimism and courage can enable me maintain my momentum as I peddle through life's sometimes obscure and murky waters.

Looking east, I bear witness to the rise of a golden sun; shining and shimmering, with the warmth and encouragement I need to replace whatever pessimism and despair lies within, with a cast-iron belief that my best is yet to come. I will, if only for one brief moment, visualise myself as a plant with its roots made up of its core essence and values whilst its shoots is a blend of its success visions, goals, dreams and aspirations.

I can learn to accept that mishaps and personal shortcomings – both within and outside of my control – are an integral part of life, teaching me not to become unduly self-critical. To the contrary, I can learn to regard every negative feeling within me as a consequence of negative occurrences; mere distractions akin to the adverse weather a plant is sometimes subjected to in the course of its growth and development.

As is the case in the botanical metamorphosis of a seed into a plant or an acorn's transition to a tree I will treat every single one of my life's achievements, present and future, as an offspring of the visions I currently harbour, rooted in, and cultivated by, my core essence and values.

There will be no sideways glance, no time to mope; neither will there be spells of self-pity because my journey of personal growth starts here and now. In my garment of personal prosperity are pockets filled with hope, optimism and courage which all feed my inner conviction that, come rain or shine, I have the fortitude and resilience to fulfil my destiny. For I believe the day a plant chooses to grow sideways, and away from the light it needs for nourishment, is the day it begins to wilt – the beginning of the end. Hence, in my pursuit of excellence, regression – backwards or sideways – will never be an option since personal advancement has become second nature to me. Yes, there will be days when things won't go in accordance with my plans and strategies. And yes, there will be moments when my progress will be 'treadmill-like' – that of a rooted motion.

Through it all, I can once again count on hope, optimism and courage to serve me that timeless reminder that success being delayed doesn't equate to it being denied. Like a juggernaut, my inner motivation will remain at its optimal best; it may be slowed down every now and again, but bringing that deep-rooted motivational force of mine to a complete halt would be impossible, even for the most extreme of life's adversities.

Opting to see opportunity in every adversity isn't – and will never be – synonymous with blind expectation; or even self-motivation based on self-deception. The ultimate aim for me is to learn to see the bigger picture in every adverse situation; from what I perceive to be bad to even the downright ugliest of situations. The reason being that the air I am able to breathe every single day – if nothing else – is one reason to be thankful and hopeful for a better day. And so long as I'm not deprived of my access to oxygen I guess every so-called personal trial and tribulation should, in comparison, be relatively easy.

Like the devastating effects of raging fires on nature's green forests, I am fully aware of how extreme personal adversity can sometimes bring immeasurable pain and hardship to human lives. Paradoxically speaking, I can see that within the vicious and diabolic nature of that very adversity there is also enor-mous potential for wisdom, personal growth and prosperity. And whilst I am under no illusion that that fire is more than capable of burning me at its worst; at its very best the heat from the same fire also has the potential to keep me warm during the harshest of cold winter nights, or cook the food I eat when I'm famished.

I can also learn to compare my personal adversity to water's curse and its gift; whilst in its uncontrolled vastness it brings to mind the words flood, tempest and tsunami, a severe lack of it, however, would mean drought and famine.

So the motivation pill for my philosophical medication today challenges me to not only see the glorious opportunity that may lie hidden in every adverse situation, but also to appreciate that the most memorable, hard-fought victories in the history of great successes, were often the ones snatched from the jaws of defeat.

Day 23

My mind is the castle that shelters my core essence of self and existence. Whilst keeping its doors shut to prevent the dust of harmful notions corrupting my thoughts, learning to keep its windows open at the right time to allow in the fresh air of innovation should also be a priority.

When my mind is well-nourished it becomes an impregnable fortress which shields it from the invasion of intrusive thoughts. Hence, my belief that nurturing my mind will steer me safely through storms of emotional upheaval; giving me balance and the stronger sense of well-being I require to handle life's day-to-day challenges. At its best, my mind can become a shining light that illuminates my path towards peace, happiness and enlightenment. Its misuse, on the other hand, would result in pain, misery and anguish – for I understand that as limitless as my mind's strengths and capabilities are, so are its frailties and vulnerabilities.

The complex nature of my mind's workings do not negate the fact that as a rational human being I can successfully navigate the path my mind takes because I alone hold the power to control the information adopted or rejected by it.

In order to lead a better quality of life marked by an enhanced, subjective well-being I will strive to find some sort of meaning in every potential setback; at the core of every adversity lies a potential opportunity for me to learn and grow.

Lying at the heart of emotional pain is the spiritual growth that can disentangle me from the tentacles of psychological barriers to my success, ranging from indecision and procrastination to inertia and a lackadaisical attitude. Today marks the beginning of freedom from mental stagnation; a day I'm once again reminded that if I so wish, I can gain mastery over my mind's activities, or do nothing and become enslaved by its weaknesses. And with such willpower and self-discipline at my disposal, I can become my mind's 'gatekeeper' – the one who, with meticulous vigilance, constantly watches over and screens through every notion, idea and perception – good and bad – looking to cross its borders. Ultimately, through my conscious decision to invest in the development of my mind, I am signing up to be the author of my present and future outcomes. And, even when those outcomes aren't favourable ones, I can learn to be at peace with my inner self by coming to terms with them – taking today's lessons forward into a new tomorrow.

Day 24

Every positive thought I create alongside every informed decision I make will be followed by a positive action and a desired outcome.

I can become a positive role model for my generation and those yet unborn. I can reinvent myself to become an influencer and a vehicle of positive change; that man who holds an ideology rooted in, and cultivated from, inherent values and belief systems hinged on all things righteous.

I can overcome every manner of obstacle that litters my path in the quest for personal success and prosperity. I can strive to emulate the men and women whom I perceive as trendsetters; the ones who have risen above adversity to relentlessly seek out their personal success and prosperity. I can work conscientiously to establish my very own unique set of principles as the foundation of moral value and core essence upon which the pillars of my future aspirations will be erected.

Even though my mind and body are separate entities, they can function as one unit if I am prepared to proactively monitor my thought patterns and how they drive my emotions and consequently influence my moods, actions and behaviours. Hence, my outcomes and individual circumstances are dependent on the quality and state of my thought patterns. And if, for whatever reason, I inadvertently limit the scope of my mind's potential through negative, self-fulfilling prophecies I can count on my inherent ability to refocus, reframe and reverse that order; for it is only by pausing, reflecting and retracing my steps that I can catapult myself back to the cusp of great achievement.

Today ushers in a new era of ambition on my part; a time to seal shut the crevices of self-doubt which can potentially dent my self-esteem and self-belief. And in its stead, I have chosen to adopt the habit of engaging in positive inner conversations of hope and optimism, complemented by the courage to act against the odds, creating uplifting thoughts and images that will guide me to the realisation of my goals, dreams, and aspirations.

Day 25

What a glass-half-empty mind may sometimes perceive as arrogance, the born optimist within me chooses to call 'firm conviction'.

If, indeed, I am serious about being fully committed to my own success and personal advancement I must embrace the idea that intelligence, technical knowledge and aptitude devoid of wisdom and a positive mental attitude would be nothing short of a futile exercise. That said, I can find solace and comfort in the fact that in whatever shapes or sizes adversity comes at me I can truly rise above it by counteracting my not so good memories of the past with the successful ones. This can be achieved by reliving and reviewing each of those moments where I excelled against the odds in order to make it from a 'bad place' to a 'very good place'. And, because I have tasted success before in unlikely situations, there is no doubt in my mind that I can accomplish this feat again. By summoning my mental skill of recall, I can trigger the memories of how I weathered those particular storms to enable me to make that transition from a 'good place' to an even 'better place'.

Even on the odd occasion when I find myself tripping or slipping, I can will myself to stand firm. Because I am encouraged by the optimistic notion that buried deep within all of my adversities are opportunities, I am choosing to see 'darkness' as a necessity in my life in order for me to fully appreciate the essence of 'light'. Of what value would the term 'success' hold in my life if not preceded by setbacks? And should I experience further knock-backs in pursuit of success I will persevere; for the will to persist and succeed against all the odds is borne out of the most compelling of my personal motivational reasons.

Recording my day-to-day struggles and corresponding victories helps to heighten my self-awareness and strengthen my self-belief that all obstacles can be surmounted.

I will relentlessly pursue all of my set goals by tuning into my 'whys' – also known as emotionally compelling reasons for wanting to succeed. And, if change is not feasible in any particular area of my life, I will learn to be at peace with the realities – adapting and, if need be, making the necessary self-adjustments in line with those realities.

Whilst the glass half-empty voice within me whispers 'flight' with frailty, its half-full counterpart strongly and fearlessly asserts 'fight'. And in terms of dealing with stressful situations that are beyond my sphere of influence, I'll first seek to avoid and, if avoidance proves futile, I will add to my resources to combat the adversity and, if that proves futile, I will aim to either adjust or adapt to the circumstances in question.

I will also aim to lead a life which embraces the notion that the genesis of most, if not all, my outcomes and circumstances – good or bad; negative or positive; the favourable and undesirable – is deeply rooted in my personal perception of the events and never the events in themselves. I can learn to understand that my personal battle to survive, and thrive, in this world will indeed be won or lost way before the first pistol is drawn, never mind fired.

I will also pay more attention to the personal interpretations and meanings I assign to every event and situation and, more importantly, recognise that how I choose to react to these circumstances will often determine the success of my coping strategies or lack of them. So, if the perception I choose to adopt when faced with a setback is grim and bleak, my coping mechanisms would equally be that of inertia and resignation. If, on the other hand, I ally myself with hope, optimism and courage, what was merely a temporary spark would gradually transform into an eternal flame of durable inner resources, enabling me to cope, regardless of the number of barricades that stand between me and success.

Day 26

No matter how much of an expert I perceive myself to be in any area of my life I will learn to exercise humility when it comes to seeking advice in the areas in which I possess little or no knowledge.

Irrespective of how brilliant a 'surgeon' I am or perceive myself to be, it would still take the expertise of another surgeon to perform a life-saving, major surgical procedure on me should I require it. For the thought of me – an expert 'surgeon' in my own right – lying on an operating table to dissect myself would be unthinkable, let alone possible.

I can successfully navigate my way through life's, sometimes hostile, territories if I learn to collaborate with others in areas in which I have limited knowledge. For how can I objectively appraise the true picture of my life if my clarity does not go beyond the frame of that very picture? Hence, the need for external input or the constructive feedback of others. For I can become open to the idea that a fresh pair of eyes brings with it a new perspective, beyond the borders of my mindset, that will enable me to make that transition to the next phase in my personal development. If, in my everyday approach to life, I learn to include a lateral 'we' way thinking with the, already in place, 'me' way of reasoning, my success would surely be a matter of 'when' and never a question of 'if'.

In the spirit of a true born optimist I will continuously advocate for, and contribute towards, a world where collaboration prevails over domination and isolation; a world where interdependency is perceived not as a sign of weakness, but a symptom of true greatness.

I can learn to appreciate that being self-motivated may not necessarily be synonymous with carrying the entire world's burdens on one's shoulders. Even though the successful individuals worthy of emulation in the world today all have peculiar traits which distinguish them from one another in terms of vision, acumen and decision making, a certain quality tends to unite them all: knowing when to be self-reliant and when to seek out external resources. I can look for, and learn from, the smartest people around; that rare species of humans who know when to put aside personal egos to syphon off knowledge from those they perceive as being smarter in specialised areas in which they find their own know-how limited. As a consequence, I'll be deriving useful insights which would help transform my areas of potential strength into that of actual strength.

To become the 'authentic' human I aspire to be, an honest form of self-analysis on my part will be required – a reflective stare at my mental mirror to objectively gauge and assess my own strengths and limitations may be the first step in the right direction. There may be nothing that empowers and motivates me more than learning from the individual who chooses to retreat into his or her 'me and me alone' cocoon in times of difficulties. By choosing to steer my life through the lenses of 'self' and 'self' alone I could be missing out on the splendour and enrichment that the spirit of collaboration brings to humankind.

As I step out from the enclave of 'self' today into the open world of 'others' my overall mentality will be to acknowledge that, even though I possess the unique potential to achieve whatever it is I set my sights upon, constantly striving to identify areas of commonalities with my fellow men and women would only add to me as a person. Building, developing and enhancing the quality of partnerships with others who have the answers to questions that I don't, may be the key to plugging that gap between merely being good and being great.

Day 27

Since I am responsible for the thoughts and emotions I create, both my happiness and external outcomes can be direct products of my internal creations.

If I learn to cultivate an awareness of my own mental processes and the ability to cut off negative streams of thought as they arise, not only will I stand a greater chance of influencing my life's direction in the future but, more importantly, what happens in the here and now.

If I do nothing then I may find myself enslaved by the fluctuations and changes in my surroundings rather than being the chief influencer of my very own domain.

I will retreat from a path characterised by the 'wait-see-and-react' mentality and, instead, pursue the one which encourages me to pre-empt, assess, and adapt when faced with challenges. That said, I can also learn to appreciate that it may be somewhat premature and delusional on my part to think that I can be right all the time in my judgement of what direction the pendulum of life swings at any point in time. One thing of which I am certain is that exhibiting courage on my part means having the courage to embrace setbacks, rather than feeling completely helpless, when it comes to my life's affairs.

From this moment on, I will put myself in a position where I can make the most of my ability to find hope, optimism and the courage to act where there seems to be none. I have no doubt that, through conscious effort and practice on my part, my mind can override the array of self-limiting thoughts and negative beliefs which sometimes pervades my mental environment. For it is only through this medium that I can have both a greater say and higher degree of influence on the events that affect my life rather than becoming eternally subservient to the sometimes cruel and unsavoury nature of that entity better known as 'fate'.

Ultimately, if I aim to make my core essence of self and existence the bedrock of my goals, dreams and aspirations, all three will most definitely need to align with each and every one of my decisions, plans of action and, ultimately, behaviours.

Day 28

What some have described as 'failure' or 'disastrous', I have chosen to accept as a mere learning curve.

Could it be possible that the absence of hope, optimism and the courage to persist on my part is what brought about my past tendency to deem setbacks as failures?

What if I choose to treat each of my setbacks, today and tomorrow, as phases on my journey and never a final destination? Perhaps an ideal starting point could be that examination I did not pass the first time, or the job opportunity which slipped through my fingers; not to mention that project I dedicated limitless time, energy and resources to, but never saw the light of the day. And what if I make a conscious effort to counteract the memory of these setbacks by recalling their successful counterparts? Or if I occasionally remind myself of the time I put my own personal needs aside in order to make a difference to the lives of others? Or recall that indelible moment that I decided to turn my back on a life of self-obsession in exchange for one of social and economic contribution? Even in areas where I perceive myself to have underperformed, provided I see beyond the 'destination' and 'finality' of such setbacks and, instead, adopt a 'vehicle' or 'means-to-an-end' outlook I will certainly prevail. Being a student of life sometimes requires me to find a positive meaning in the value of not getting things right the first time, no matter how hard that may seem. For with setbacks comes maturity, personal growth, and wisdom; all of which would enhance my future performance and productivity.

Day 29

Regardless of the negative information presented to me externally I am ultimately responsible for what drives and influences me internally and what does not.

I am aware that, as exciting and exhilarating a place the world is, there is no discounting its drawbacks in the form of negative information which has the propensity to instil in me a sense of despair. From economic issues such as job insecurities, rises in the cost of living and poverty, to social malaise such as intolerance, discrimination and hatred towards innocent people. These are mere snippets of the daily challenges human beings face on a day-to-day basis and one of the many obstacles I would need to overcome in order to make that transition from who I am to the person I aim to become. And whilst I may trip up and fall into a ditch of self-deceit by thinking for one minute that I can fix the world's problems, I remain secure in the knowledge that I can give humankind one less thing to worry about by doing my utmost to maximise my own potential. By taking personal responsibility of identifying, harnessing and developing my talents, I can contribute my quota to the advancement of my community and beyond.

Whilst the hope within me instils me with courage by reminding me of how I've survived the grimmest of life's realities, my optimism presents me with the necessary pathway to reaching the very pinnacle of my potential. In all of this, there will always be two choices available to me: to remain an integral part of the problem or to be the solution through connecting with my inner resources to become an actual vehicle for positive change.

Through the medium of my daily positive inner conversations I remain assured that the physical world around me, as represented by negative events, situations and circumstances, can be subservient to the inner dictates of my mind if I so will it. For the majority of the negative elements in my life are none other than my mind's own creations as dictated by my past and present experiences and my physical and psychological environments. And because I choose to believe that a 'creator' should have some – if not absolute – measure of control over the 'created', it seems absurd that I should forever be enslaved to events rather than being in control of my reaction to them.

So, moving forward, I will acknowledge the presence of the vast amount of untapped potential resident within me. And like a slumbering giant perennially waiting to be jolted into life, this inner colossus will eventually enable me take my rightful place in the esteemed company of other great men and women whose vision is to leave behind a better world than the one we were born into.

Day 30

Affluence and poverty might be two different destinations but they require one state of mind to reach; I alone wield the mental power to guide my life in either one of those two directions.

I will begin this morning by inculcating in me a balanced notion of wealth and poverty. I will strive to find a subjective definition of the term 'success' that works well for me and not necessarily accept the widely popular notion that being successful always has to be associated with material possessions or socio-economic status. I will devote my time and inner resources to imbibing a new set of beliefs which subscribe to the idea that even if I fall short of the acceptable 'success standards' promoted by society, this won't make me any less successful than the next man or woman. I can learn to develop for myself my very own working definition of being successful, financially sound and wealthy. A personal definition which aligns with the idea that, provided my needs in life are met and I am able to make many a positive contribution to the lives of the less fortunate, the line of distinction between me and those society chooses to class as 'affluent' will become somewhat negligible. And rather than see myself repeating the same error of using the accomplishments of others as some sort of 'success barometer' to gauge the progress I'm making in life, I can choose to pause and deeply reflect on what the term 'being successful' genuinely means to me.

Against the odds, I remain assured in my inner conviction that the words 'success' and 'happiness' are, and will continue to be, what I decree them to personally mean to me, and never in line with the expectations of others. Upon reflection of my life's early experiences, orientation, current circumstances and my future aspirations I am filled with hope and optimism for what my future holds. Besides, if my personal history of trials, pain, joy, setbacks and rewards bears little, or no, semblance to those of others, what gives me – or anyone else for that matter – the right to compare my aspirations to that of the next man or woman?

In relation to money; rather than see a lack of, or insufficient amount of it, as making me 'poor' perhaps, I could learn to substitute that term with me being in 'financial transition'. For whilst proclaiming my financial situation as 'poor' projects a tone of finality and resignation in the matter, believing I'm in financial transition, on the other hand, reminds me that I'm merely experiencing an adverse phase which, with the right mental attitude and the courage to effect the necessary changes, will come to an end sooner rather than later. And I do believe that if my mind embraces the 'transition' definition of financial insufficiency like any other challenge in life, it opens up doors of lateral and divergent thinking – the vehicles I need to transform my unpleasant circumstances into a desired outcome. On the contrary, the term 'poverty' suggests to me a permanent state which would only lead my mind into passively surrendering to the 'machinations' of external circumstances rather than proactively searching for lasting solutions.

If there is one enduring lesson I have chosen to take away from today it is how the physical manifestations of terms such as 'poverty' and 'wealth' all originate from my mind's perceptions, and the personal meanings I choose to assign to each of my experiences. Poised in anticipation of the limitless opportunities and possibilities my future promises, I will ensure that my working definition of the word 'success' will not be exclusive to the world of material possessions alone. My personal success will be defined by an appraisal of my overall well-being as a human being – my personal perception of the distance (if any) between my life's current circumstances and my ideals. I can begin to set new personal goals aimed at bringing my life's realities in harmony with its potential – and so long as there is a minimal, or non-existent, discrepancy between the two, the notion of wealth and subjective happiness – albeit two separate entities – will become one reality in my life.

Day 31

Not only will I celebrate my personal achievements of yesterday, I will build on those successes for today and tomorrow. As for the setbacks of yesterday and today, I will learn from them, rather than continuously dwell on them.

Regardless of my past and present setbacks or shortcomings, I can learn to instil within me a sense of gratitude and appreciation for my achievements and the obstacles I've successfully overcome.

I can lead a life that willingly gives to others with little, or no, expectation of reward as the primary motivation for my giving in the first instance. From my being there for a friend or family member in their time need, to my display of random acts of kindness towards total strangers, I can bring down the 'self alone' borders and embrace a personal culture of altruism.

I can begin to reorientate myself with the notion that exhibiting selfless acts, without the expectation of getting something back in return, can, in itself, open up a pathway to my personal growth and prosperity. I can also learn to embrace certain concepts that contribute towards my well-being, beyond merely making me feel good, to actually being and staying good. From self-nurturing behaviours that can help insulate my psychological well-being from the tentacles of depression, despair, and negative stress, to exuding altruistic qualities which will release me from the cocoon of 'self' and transport me to the open world of 'others' around me. If my personal accomplishments were seeds, watering them day in, day out, in the garden of my mind, will enable them to grow from acorns to plants, and eventually trees. And by trees, I mean growing into my very own personal 'achievement tree'.

This 'achievement tree' of mine is the medium through which I am able to identify resources within myself in those dark spells of my life when I'm all alone trying to navigate life's perilous terrain. A tree whose leaves of hope, optimism and the courage to act constantly whisper comforting words to me when blown by the wind of adverse change; soothing words that say to me, 'You've done it before, and you can most definitely do it again if only you choose to believe.'

With this in mind, I will desist from treating my 'achievement tree' like a Christmas tree; the symbolic meaning of my 'achievement tree' won't be reduced to that of mere decoration designed to be put up before the 25th day of December each year, only to be taken down by January. Unlike a traditional Christmas tree, my 'achievement tree' will be displayed at the forefront of mind all year round in order for my inner motivation to achieve greater things and be sustained and enhanced.

This 'achievement tree', for me, represents self-esteem, self-empowerment and an acknowledgement of my triumphs in the face of life's endless trials and challenges; it will be an embodiment of inner strength that will continue to define my individuality, advancement of self and my significant positive contribution to the world of others.

Day 32

Whilst I may derive some degree of inner satisfaction from the things I possess or can call my own, it is the things I am able to overlook or live without that serve as a true measure of my character.

Today brings with it another opportunity to instil within me a short-term, delayed gratification mentality in order to realise my long-term goals, dreams and aspirations.

I can acknowledge that for me to harbour inner peace and tranquility in a world where the prevailing attitude to life seems to be a culture of 'having-it-now and paying-the-price-later', I can review both my thinking and behavioural patterns. I can play an integral part in building communities and societies whilst simultaneously challenging the self-limiting ideas and negativity which sometimes come from the very same societies I am dedicated to serving.

From its doldrums of materialism I – alongside other born optimists – can help certain sections of society attain a paradigm shift which would distance itself from unwittingly defining a man or woman by their visual worth as against the content of their deeds and character.

For my part, I will strive to lead a life showcasing my values ahead of my perceived assets; be it the value of my bank balance or material possessions. I will aim for an 'authentic' life at the expense of one merely concocted for the cameras; and choose a meaningful life over one underlined by mere pleasurable existence. And, in every way possible, I will choose a life of 'being and staying' good over that of merely 'feeling' good.

Whilst how 'I am' is many a time influenced by how 'I feel', it doesn't necessarily make the two synonymous or identical. And even when I work diligently to acquire meaningful assets in my life, such acquisitions will never be for the mere sake of acquisitions in themselves, but to serve a higher purpose, geared towards enhancing the quality of not just my life but, more significantly, those of others.

With regards to the things I already have, I can learn to appreciate them more for what I possess serves as both the foundation and building blocks for those things I am yet to possess, achieve or acquire. And, in relation to what I have and what I am yet to acquire, I know I can learn to merge the notions of present moment contentment and inner peace with those needs I aspire to in the future.

In taking my first few steps towards change, I can begin to appreciate the little things that make my life and those of others around me worthwhile without necessarily being enslaved by, or subservient to, the very same things.

Day 33

Every ailment of dejection and despondency that may come my way will be met with the remedies of positive attitude and resolute determination.

There will be periods in my life when, rather than seeing a promising future with only a cluster of dark clouds surrounding me, I see instead days when bleakness seems to usurp any glimmer of hope, optimism and courage. Should I be moved? Or perhaps simply bury my head in the sands of self-pity in the expectation that, without me having to act, the very same adversities would, all of a sudden, evaporate into thin air? Or conversely speaking, I can choose to dig dip into my inner reservoirs of fortitude and resilience for answers. And, even if I initially struggle to find a positive meaning in these tough situations, I can learn to find some sort of meaning.

Whilst it is a given that I am bound to encounter negative stress that emanates from my own thoughts and emotions, in my interaction with other people, and with adverse situations in general, I can choose calmness, composure and focus over chaos and irascibility. There will also be days when I experience mild to moderate forms of negative stress (in relation to adversity) to even the traumatic types which have the propensity to change the course of my life forever.

Regardless of the hardships I am confronted with, waking up to the gift of life each morning is, and always will be, a valid reason to remain thankful.

By being alive I am blessed with an invaluable wealth of wisdom in every lesson learnt on the way to personal prosperity.

Life's tempest may occasionally rob me of my rights and freedoms to do or achieve certain things at certain times; however, if there is one thing it cannot deprive me of, it is my right to choose my own perception (of the situation), my attitude and, ultimately, my reaction to such difficulties. For not only does the attitude I choose during the most trying of times remain an exclusive right in terms of my personal choices, it also happens to be one conduct I alone can determine. And whilst the personal aim is to lead a life which is in congruence with my goals, dreams and aspirations, I will learn to do so within reason and not at the expense of my subjective well-being and true happiness. For a 'peaceful penny' may, in the longer term, prove to be more beneficial to my mental well-being than a 'problematic pound sterling'.

If my life was a kitchen, I, and I alone, would be its 'head chef', having the final word on what ingredients would make up the dishes. Every single cooking instruction would be my call; from the quantity of seasoning to the amount of time set for my pot's content to either boil or simmer.

Day 34

The worst kind of limitation for me would be that which has the word 'self' as its prefix.

If self-limitation is a destination, then the path leading to it is one worthy of deviating from considering I have chosen self-actualisation as the ultimate path of choice in the fulfilment of my life's purpose.

Not only are my behaviours and circumstances, more often than not, tied to the thoughts and emotions I generate, they are also rooted in the core beliefs I have for long held about myself, others and life in general. I can, however, through mental rehearsals followed by constant practice choose to free myself from the stifling parameters of these self-limiting beliefs. If my beliefs are always hinged on trepidation and the anticipation of failure, there is a great possibility that this negative theme in my subconscious will gravitate me towards the very unsavoury thoughts, negative actions, behaviours, decisions and, ultimately, outcomes I set out to avoid in the first instance.

Rather than capitulate to pressure when the going seems unbearable, I can activate the emotional content of my personal motivational reason(s) for needing to succeed in whatever undertaking to boost momentum in the direction of success.

Should self-limiting, intrusive thoughts invade the borders of my mind, owing to the negative stress and adversity life brings my way, I can, prior to any knee-jerk reactions and decisions, self-monitor these thoughts, counterbalancing the good with the bad. And, should I find myself struggling to find a positive meaning in the whole experience, I will assign the terms 'phase', 'transition' and 'pit stop' to experience in my overall journey towards reaching my goals. For every single time my thoughts and my perceptions choose not to see beyond the barricades which the word 'impossible' erect before me, I automatically create for myself a self-limiting response which deprives me of the lateral and divergent thinking needed to find solutions.

If there is one enduring lesson I choose to take away from today's inner conversation, it is how – willingly or unwittingly – allowing self-limiting thoughts to permeate my consciousness can restrict my life's options; for with limited options comes limited actions which, in turn, equals zero results.

Day 35

If my vision were a blank canvas, my motivational reason for wanting to succeed would be its paint whilst my timescale and plan of action the paint brushes.

I understand that, regardless of how powerful my visualisation is, or how positive my inner conversations are, they would be of little, or no, significance if I fail to match them with day-to-day actions. I understand that the art of visualisation, even when followed with positive self-talk, that is devoid of actualisation is lacking in substance unless I inject an element of execution into it. Needless to say, even though 'feeling', 'thinking', 'seeing' and 'believing' my way to success are great habits for me to have, none comes close to actually 'doing'.

In the absence of day-to-day actions, my goals and visions would be stillborn. For these inner visions, dreams and positive affirmations that I harbour are all siblings nurtured by a single parent called 'hope', which, in itself, thrives on faith and fantasy. Hope, in isolation, however, is but one aspect of desired expectation which can only carry both me and my future aspirations so far on its frail legs and feeble shoulders. For hope not only comes with a degree of uncertainty, it also lacks clear and concrete pathways leading to the realisation of the desired expectation. For my hope to be transformed to a more solid entity, it requires, on my part, a conscious metamorphosis into optimism. Unlike hope, optimism brings with it clear proactive strategies to help turn my vision, goals and objectives, into reality. Whilst the hope within me is only necessary for my survival and self-preservation in times of adversity, optimism is necessary for both my personal growth and the fulfilment of my potential. For if I cling on to hope alone as the sole vehicle that transports me from where I currently am in my life to that very place I aspire to be, it is most likely that those dreams and aspirations would begin to wilt before my eyes, even before they've had the chance to germinate, let alone blossom.

Changing my situation is a resolve that will have to come from within me and not be enforced upon me externally; for it is the emotional content of the personal 'whys' behind my wanting to succeed in life that insulates my aspirations against the prospect of failing. And it won't really matter to me how swift or slow this change is for I know that success being delayed does not necessarily equate to success being denied. What matters most to me is emotional recognition of the need and desire to pursue my dreams vigorously to the very end, and not necessarily how soon this comes to fruition.

By creating thoughts and exhibiting particular behaviours congruent with my core essence and values on a regular basis, I am confident that achieving my goals will no longer be a hopeful scenario of 'if' I get there, but more of an optimistic case of 'when' I get there.

So, going forward, whatever goal, dream or aspiration I visualise, rather than sit and anticipate change I can become the actual vehicle of change through the relentless focus of my mind and the conscientious work of my hands.

Day 36

All the contrived negativity, skepticism and cynicism thrown my way will have no bearing on the shining nuggets of innovative ideas my mind can generate.

I firmly believe that if there is one true force capable of derailing my goals, dreams, and aspirations in life it would be none other than the reflection that stares right back at me when I gaze into the mirror. I'd like to believe that, as long as I'm able to overcome the self-generated barricades in the way of my own success – such as self-doubt, fear and anxiety, the ones that have been physically erected in front of me by external factors will never keep me up at night with worry.

I acknowledge that my life may be beset with its very own unique set of challenges; at best, the type that push me to be the very best I can be and, at worst, the ones that incapacitate me. Life's numerous negative stresses threaten to not only scupper my hope for a brighter day, but also obliterate every trait of optimism I hold for the for the future. Whilst hope is like a ray of light that pierces through each dark tunnel in my life, illuminating my path, it is my optimism that presents me with the map and compass to guide me to personal prosperity.

I am under no illusion that reaching my desired destination in life will not be straightforward, for there will be human and inanimate factors that attempt to scupper my plans, ideas and strategies, from time to time. Along the way, I am certain to meet that certain type of men and women whose primary mission is to discourage me at every opportunity and pour scorn on my way of thinking, because my way of doing things is a sharp departure from what's deemed as the accepted standard in society. Through it all, I will neither allow myself to be moved nor become a slave to the fear and trepidation that arises from the backlash associated with turning my back on the 'herd' mentality – for I have chosen to sacrifice transitory 'popularity' for durable 'authenticity'. Rather than working aimlessly to change the opinions of others, or their behaviour towards me, I will, instead, channel that very energy towards working on my own thoughts, emotions, attitude and behaviour. For it is easier to shape my reactions constructively in relation to the negativity directed towards me by others than to attempt the futile task of trying to change the way others think or behave.

With regard to human beings, and our behaviour towards one another, I can simply choose to accept that we are all products of our core values (imbibed through our early experiences) which, in turn, shape our assumptions about life and other people. And for the simple fact that we seldom have easy access to those core values, addressing or changing those thoughts and behaviours overnight becomes problematic; by focusing on improving my own values and corresponding behaviour puts me in a better position to influence others around me.

I alone will have the final word in ensuring that my goals, dreams and aspirations make it through the dark tunnel of life to the shining horizon that lies ahead of me. As I've saddled myself with the personal responsibility of being the captain of my life's vessel of dreams, the responsibility for the safe navigation of this vessel to the shore of reality lies with me and no one else.

Furthermore, I can choose to stay afloat through fortitude, perseverance and resolute determination in the face of every negative criticism, or sink by succumbing to the turbulence created.

In light of what I aim to achieve in life, I will choose personal responsibility, regardless of the toxic opinion that comes from some quarters; for the attitude I adopt in relation to what is attributed to me by others is of more significance and value than the actual attribution in itself.

Day 37

My choice of success over failure is no different from my choice of delicacies at a buffet; what goes on my plate is no one else's responsibility but mine.

If I pay closer attention to the phenomenon of cause and effect I will come to appreciate that one event hardly ever occurs in isolation of other events. For I am bound to get out of life what I consciously put into it in terms of the effort and time I devote to self-improvement, the realisation of my dreams and the role I play in helping to enhance the quality of other people's lives.

From the minute I wake up, to the moment I lay down to sleep at night, I can set aside a penny of resourcefulness each single day for my life's piggy bank. I can learn to make the transition from being a mere disciple of hope to being an ambassador of optimism. One who grows from being a visionary armed with the question 'what?' to that innovator who includes 'when?', 'how?' and 'why?' to his stream of consciousness. I can rise to become that individual who has taken it upon himself to assume the responsibility of no longer being a mere passenger in life's vehicle, but the actual driver.

Even though I'm blessed with a natural right to my own personal choices and decisions I am also conscious that the right to self-fulfilment which I possess comes with a social responsibility not to infringe upon the right to self-fulfilment which the next man and woman also possess.

Day 38

I understand the occasional need for a short-term disruption in order to achieve long-term progression.

I will neither be obsessed with, nor overwhelmed by, the occasional setbacks or instability that comes hand in hand with everyday struggle. I will be mindful of how a defeatist mentality has the propensity to impede my ability to recognise that the knock-backs of yesterday and today can be subservient to the potential success of tomorrow.

For me to advance there may be a need for me to take measured strides from that 'dark place' in my life towards a brighter horizon by learning from my mistakes and the mistakes of others. I know there will be days when my attempts to be self-driven may prove futile owing to the nature of the hardships, or genuine life traumas, I may encounter. I also know that when those days do come around not only will I do well to remind myself of the precious gift of life itself that I have been blessed with, but also seek out external resources, whilst waiting on my inner strength to kick in. And whilst I am aware it may be a struggle, at first, to find any kind of meaning in these situations (let alone positive ones), by holding on tight to courage, and not giving up or giving in, victory would surely be but a matter of time. For I strongly believe that at the heart of each of my adversities lies an opportunity to learn, grow and excel in every facet of my life.

I can also learn that, in order for me to fully appreciate the value of my life's positives, I need to come to terms with its setbacks by being at peace with them – for the beauty of any light I see is only reinforced and made more special by memories of my treading through darkness. And even when life's challenges and hardships threaten to blur my vision of a brighter tomorrow, I can build and enhance my inner motivation by reminding myself that, regardless of how 'bad' I deem my status, there is always a 'worse' situation in life. So long as I'm willing to try, I can connect with positive inner resources, building optimism and courage along the way, and identify the things that ensure 'bad' does not deteriorate to 'worse'.

To attain the true level of success I crave, I must be open to the idea that it may come with a phase of extreme regression before any progression is imminent. My personal success will not only be measured by the things I possess, or have been able to achieve, but, more significantly, those things I have been able to do or live without for long-lasting success is an offspring of delayed gratification.

Perhaps my being disillusioned with life in general is sometimes as a result of constantly seeing a setback or disappointment as an end in itself rather than a means to an end. And rather than choosing to treat the disruptions that come with human existence with a tone of finality, I can choose to perceive them as integral phase in my attainment of a successful outcome. There will be no shortcuts or quick fixes on my journey towards excellence; for this is a path meant for that spirit of fortitude resident within me – that resilient force goading me on in the fight for my future and that of others. To make this vision a reality I am prepared to forfeit instant short-term pleasure, embracing transitory pain along the way, in order to ultimately achieve the long-term gains and rewards I believe I truly deserve.

Beyond 'self' I am also prepared to lead what I personally believe to be the 'authentic' life. For I can learn to make the transition from self-preservation and self-nurture to focus on activities and projects aimed at making a lasting positive contribution to humankind. I am prepared to look at the bigger picture of life, rather than taking a myopic view of situations and events. For I know that a reorientation of my mindset towards embracing self-nurture and altruism is the clearest path yet to making the attainment of genuine happiness and inner peace a reality, rather than a mere figment of my fantasies.

Day 39

I have chosen not to allow the disappointments of yesterday mar the potential successes of today and tomorrow.

If I maintain a despondent and gloomy perception of yesterday's disappointments emanating from life's numerous knockbacks, not only can this attitude negatively impact my overall well-being, it can also obstruct my quest for personal success. So rather than pay setbacks the wrong kind of attention, I can learn to see each adversity as my very own launch pad in the attainment of excellence.

The tougher the going gets the more relentless I will be in reinforcing within me the born optimist mantra which asserts that, so long as I'm alive to witness the dawn of every brand new day, I stand as good a chance as anyone of transforming each of my visions of success and personal prosperity into reality.

I can begin to channel my focus on amending my thinking style from that of pessimism to one of hope and optimism. Rather than being engaged in an obsessive pursuit of radical lifestyle changes I can, one day at a time, work on tweaking my thought style first. For trying to change certain negative behaviours, without first attempting to review the corresponding negative thought patterns, would yield little, or no, dividends towards the constructive change in personality I seek.

Whilst I accept that, with the right level of self-discipline and determination, a lifestyle change for me wouldn't be an impossible feat, I am also aware that changing my style of thinking first would make the process of constructively changing my personality a lot easier. Can I really find any reward in expending my emotional energy on past irrevocable occurrences at the expense of the present and the things that are yet to be? Would doing this not be a terrible waste of inner resources and, ultimately, potential on my part? What if I consciously decide to cultivate the habit of uttering the positive inner monologue of 'Even though I know things did not go as planned yesterday and today, tomorrow still presents me with ample opportunities to make it right!'? And, what if making self-affirming proclamations on a day-to-day basis, regardless of the magnitude of the hardships I face, goes a long way in aligning the positivity of my thoughts with my behaviour, actions, decisions and eventual outcomes?

Today heralds the beginning of a new era for me; when the majority of my focus will be on clearing my mind of its cobwebs of doom, which have for long incarcerated its creativity and innovation. For now is the moment to rid my mind of despondency and, replace it with hope, optimism, and possibility, all of which have been presented to me through the courage to act and pursue my dreams. It may take nothing more on my part but a firm resolve – backed by the courage to act – for my vision of a better tomorrow to become a reality. Plus, the person I have now become understands that the most effective remedy for the painful memories of my past mistakes and setbacks, is to treat each and every one of them as experiences to learn from, rather than to dwell on.

Day 40

Irrespective of the negative energy around me, be it in terms of what is said or heard, I will remain focused on the task at hand; energised by the enthralling nature of the mission that lies ahead.

What if one of the many causes of my pain, fear, and discontent might be excessive emotional and physical attachment to the world around me? What if I begin to treat the so-called 'pleasures' or 'necessities' of life as mere 'vehicles' – a means to an end rather than an end in itself? Or what if every brand new day is judiciously used in appreciating more of where I am and aspire to be, and less of where I once was and how it could have been? And what if I spend more time and energy being in the moment, whilst also projecting for the future, as opposed to living everyday with my eyes obsessively glued to life's rear-view mirror?

I can embrace the spirit of individuality, single-mindedness and autonomy in my approach to doing the things which I find congruent with my core values. And even when some ill-informed sections of society choose to interpret my uncompromising attitude towards the values I hold dear as 'weak' or 'weird', I can simply smile to myself whilst repeating one of my many self-motivational inner monologues. That very monologue that reminds me that, what the world may sometimes class as 'weird' or 'weak', could in fact be something 'unique' ; a pathway to my very own personal prosperity. I know that being scorned or ridiculed is the price I sometimes have to pay for choosing to take the road less travelled, as opposed to following the wider and more popular path - also known as 'Herd Avenue'. As for the word 'majority', it does not necessarily equate to prosperity, the same way 'popularity' doesn't always align with 'authenticity'.

As I move through this fortieth day on my mission to reach the lofty heights of my aspirations, I will make a concerted effort to remember that true inner peace and genuine happiness isn't necessarily rooted in public approval of my ideas or actions but hinged upon an objective self-appraisal of my own life. Whilst victories in the court of public opinion (approval by others) might be great for my ego, it is the private victories (approval of self) in the corridors of my mind that are priceless – for I see self-acceptance as a prerequisite for inner contentment and genuine happiness. External validation (popularity) is like a temporary spark that comes on one minute only to be extinguished the next, owing to the, sometimes, breathtaking pace at which public perception changes. However, inner validation and genuineness (authenticity) will, for me, represent a long-lasting, robust flame that glows in the dark and transcends time.

Day 41

The more I learn to acknowledge and celebrate my achievements of the past and present, the more motivated and better equipped I will be in overcoming any future obstacle.

I can learn to appreciate that, sometimes, the best kind of horn to blow is my very own. How else can I come to terms with the adversities, trials and tribulations I face on a daily basis without stark reminders of the numerous 'Goliaths' of my past that I've successfully slain? The self-acknowledgement of my conquests may be viewed by some as 'egotism' and 'conceit'; or even 'arrogance' and 'self-importance'. The main question, however, is if a little bit of self-appreciation on my part in terms of my accomplishments – big and small – should be a quality to shy away from? For one of the most realistic ways for me to build and enhance the inner motivation needed to overcome challenges is rooted in the sincere and open recognition of not just what I've been able to do to get to where I am today, but what I continue to do to improve on my current status.

When I stare in the mirrors of my mind, I can either choose to see limitations or possibilities and opportunities. Likewise, I could exude incessant anxiety over my worst fear and events yet to materialise, rather than remain self-assured and convinced in the notion that, since I've scaled seemingly insurmountable problems before, present and future concerns should not really be a source of trepidation. Be it as it may, if the images I project for my future do not in any way conform to my present day reality, I will make concerted efforts to practice generating new thoughts that reflect my goals; describing them, and acting on them, until a bridge is erected between the spot I occupy today and that very place I aspire to reach tomorrow.

And because I am of the firm belief that my mental rehearsals (the art of acting out or describing in detail how I aim to accomplish my set goals) sets the right kind of tone for actual execution of my visions, I will endeavour to continue describing my goals to myself, reinforcing the 'whys' for wanting to achieve them even when the 'how' remains a mystery to me. And so long as I can answer the questions of 'what' (needs to be accomplished) and 'why' (it needs to be achieved) in relation to my goals, dreams and aspirations, there really should not be any doubt in my heart and mind that the 'how' will come in due course.

Regardless of the nature of the challenges and hardships I have had to endure, I will continue to harbour the conviction that as long as I do not slumber, my breakthrough is almost at hand. For I can draw inspiration from every rough stone once buried and forgotten by time but now excavated from the muddiest of trenches and polished into the finest of diamonds.

Day 42

No matter what my achievements in life are, I will never be complacent. For complacency is like having a warm and soothing rug beneath my feet; the longer I stand on that rug the less prepared I will be when abruptly pulled from underneath me.

Each one of my life's accomplishments can serve as the motivational platform I need to reach even greater heights.

I am aware that it may be one thing drawing inspiration and self-belief from yesterday's breakthroughs, it is quite another avoiding the trap of being overly obsessed with my past to the extent of losing sight of the work needed to achieve greater successes in the future.

If there is one lesson I can learn from the visionaries and achievers in a variety of fields – be it in business, sport and entertainment, or even politics and philanthropy – who have had to overcome many obstacles in order to make the world a better place, it is how they continuously strive to attain greater heights despite the magnitude of success they have already attained. Hence, it isn't what I have achieved, or am currently striving to achieve, that counts but my ability to continue to seek self-improvement in all that I do and what I am still capable of sharing with the world in terms of my natural talents and abilities.

I know how tempting it is to take a back-seat and rest on my laurels with the perception that my life's version of 'Mount Everest' has being successfully surmounted. I will also be mindful of how Herculean a task it is to remain motivated and build on my success when the adulation (of my peers), accolades and rewards which come with the territory all begin to arrive on my doorstep. Being unprepared for this phase of success at its infancy can result in complacency, the arch nemesis of self-progression. So long as my inner motivation to excel remains intact, fighting off the urge to remain complacent every single day will become my new reality, and not just a possibility. Rather than choosing to see every milestone and achievement in my life as a 'thus far and no farther' kind of accomplishment, I can treat these successes as mere pit stops for refuelling purposes only; a phase for reflection, recharging of the batteries and proceeding to the next stop in my pursuit of the next goal, the next dream, and the next aspiration.

With a proactive mentality I can consciously become immune to the malaise of inertia and spiritual decay – both of which are an offspring of complacency. Not only would my giving in to self-limiting behaviours impede my ability to develop, it also has the propensity to negatively impact my contribution to society as a whole.

This forty-second day of my journey towards achieving the seemingly impossible will see me become an active contributor to the progress of humankind, and not that man who indolently snoozes through the process of positive change. After all, a society in which men and women habitually oversleep is one that will soon decline into poverty.

Day 43

Regardless of the often competitive nature of life's race track the bulk of my energy will be channelled towards keeping within my lane and excelling in my own performance.

Because I'm all too aware of how divided attention and distractions on my part can be stifling to my progress in life, I have earmarked today as the day I jettison the self-limiting habit of incessantly peeping over my shoulder. For I know that being obsessively glued to my rear-view mirror on life's race track – to catch a glimpse of where my peers are positioned – is in itself a recipe for catastrophe in my quest for success.

Perhaps I need to understand that, in the realm of success and achievement, only one thing counts: a single-minded and objective appraisal of the distance between where I am and where I need to be. Regardless of what I do, or whatever routes I choose to navigate in the course of reaching my set goals, I can only truly achieve this with one mind and firm conviction. In the course of my journey, I may encounter tasks and challenges with the propensity to stretch me beyond my own limits – in the face of this very adversity it is still possible to find the courage to persist through the pain; for if I fail to believe in my own inner strengths to overcome challenges why should anyone else believe in me?

As for double-mindedness, there is no point entertaining such, as this state of mind is symptomatic of uncertainty and indecision; precursors to apathy and, eventually, inaction.
If the best ideas and ingenious concepts that have shaped the modern world were born from the gut instincts and visions of men and women like me, what holds me back from emulating

such exemplary individuals? By opting for internally-derived motivation for change rather than being solely dependent on motivation that has been externally-imposed upon me, I remain confident that my drive to succeed can be sustainable for many years to come. That said, prioritising the use of inner resources over those without does not necessarily negate the need for me to collaborate or seek partnerships with others.

For I can appreciate that it is only through calling on external resources in areas where my knowledge is inadequate or limited I can add to my personal resources in the accomplishment of my goals.

Considering that I'm part of a world where humans are diverse in their orientation, background and experiences, not to mention in the nature of their adversities, would there really be any sense in me tailoring the solutions of others to my own personal challenges which are by no means identical to that of the next man and woman? Or, is it not conceivable that by first consulting my very own inner resources, the concepts of lateral thinking and problem-solving will automatically become accessible to me time and time again?

Whilst today seems to have presented me with more questions than answers, there may be one crucial lesson I am choosing to take away: prior to looking for answers to my life's burning questions in distant lands perhaps the ideal place to start would be at my own very own doorstep.

Day 44

My self-belief, determination and actions are the foundations upon which the virtual dreams in my life are transformed into actual things.

Resolute determination, matched by an appropriate plan of action, will be integral to the actualisation of my future aspirations. My inner vision of success, through hope and optimism, can serve as a useful platform for achieving my lifelong goals. For this inner vision also empowers me by helping me to find the, often elusive, courage that I need to brave all kinds of adverse situations on my march to victory, even when my so-called 'common-sense' occasionally tries to dissuade me from the cause.

Whatever my aspirations, if devoid of self-belief, it would be like constructing a house of cards with a view to seeking refuge from life's storms within it. And of what use is my self-belief if, at the slightest setback, the determination to persevere deserts me?

Within me lies an impregnable fortress of fortitude which towers over all my personal adversities; a fortress built on a pride-filled heritage of personal triumphs and memories of success. Memories ranging from the battles and challenges I've braved in reaching the place where I am today, to the treacherous terrains that I have traversed in my refusal to capitulate to life's hardships. Surely, it is this determined spirit of courage under pressure and perseverance that has enabled me to endure when there seemed to be no solution. And even if the pain I experience is of the protracted nature, my vision of long-term gain will give me that unquenchable thirst to excel; the driving force that keeps getting me out of bed each morning.

With regards to my well-being; not only are my thoughts and emotions products of my mind, my corresponding behaviour, decisions and actions are all subservient to it. And even though I acknowledge that the physical and mental entities of my life will sometimes act in isolation to one another they are still interlinked with my mind. For my mind is the ultimate 'conductor' of music that dictates every rhythm of my life in an orchestra of diverse occurrences and situations.

I know that I am endowed with the natural ability to self-generate my very own successes. I also know that I have what it takes to inculcate within my mind the self-belief, determination and, more importantly, the will, to proactively pursue and actualise my own visions of the future. For I am the author of my own visions and, therefore, need to be in control of the path each of my visions follows in becoming a reality. Rather than passively reacting to situations outside of my influence, I can take time out to sit back, relax and remind myself that I hold the power to craft an impregnable fortress out of, what may otherwise have been, mere 'sandcastles' when it comes to facing life's adversities.

Day 45

To survive, I will keep up the fight; never taking flight or giving in to fright. And in order to thrive, I will persist on and never desist from.

The inner motivation vehicle I have chosen to board today is that of endurance and persistence – the art of being subtle in my overall approach without compromising my inherent indomitable spirit which springs into life when faced with life's obstacles.

I can clothe my essence in the armour-like skin of a rhinoceros to withstand life's external pressures, yet also allow it to flow gracefully like an eternal stream constantly adapting to the numerous objects in its path. Flowing ceaselessly, this core essence of mine will continue to find multiple pathways to its ultimate destination regardless of obstructions – rocks, fences, boulders and all.

Not only will my motivational reason for seeking to accomplish every goal I set myself be compelling, it will also be steeped in emotional significance. For when all else fails, the personal 'whys' for wanting to fulfil my life's potential will serve as my solitary source of sustenance, continuously goading me on towards the very place I aspire to be. And whilst meeting or exceeding my own set targets can evoke in me both a feeling of self-worth and a sense of achievement, I will remain open to learning from transitory setbacks and missed past targets, rather than regarding such situations as 'failures'.

Invoking that born optimist spirit within me, once again, would mean learning to explore my life's limitless possibilities. By

114

adopting a positive, can-do mindset I am able to approach new challenges and unpleasant scenarios like some sort of 'success archaeologist' whose life's mission is to exhume nuggets of wisdom and opportunity buried within each rubble of life's adversity. For viewing my life through the bifocal lenses of my disappointments alone, is to unwittingly open up a floodgate of further disappointments.

From this day on, there will be no fictional 'pies in the sky' for me when it comes to reaching those lofty goals I aim for. And since I deem myself fully prepared for this bumpy ride I will be under no illusion that this journey will be easy, for it is a given that the path leading to success is sometimes fraught with peril of every kind imaginable; from 'wolves' lurking in the shadows disguised as 'sheep', to camouflaged serpents in the undergrowth. Come what may, I am prepared to face all of my adversaries head on, armed with a flame of inner belief which constantly reassures me that my victory will, in time, be assured. And when my adversaries threaten to devour my dreams, I can do well to remind myself that the greatest obstacle standing between where I am and the place I aspire to be isn't necessarily threats from the outside world, but that which in itself is resident within me.

As today draws to an end, let me appreciate that the insight and clarity I have acquired will help me accept that my most formidable adversary is none other than that which is of my very own creation: self-doubt.

Day 46

In every show of strength lies a flaw and in every flaw lies a potential for strength; I will keep building on my strengths each passing day until my flaws become insignificant in comparison to my strengths.

The motivational pill for my soul's consumption today simply encourages me to embrace my human make-up as a paradoxical interplay of both capabilities and vulnerabilities. For me to attain both spiritual and mental growth, perhaps, it is important that I learn the art of self-acceptance. For I now believe that it is only by pursuing the pathway leading to an 'authentic' life and creating an environment within conducive to making me feel comfortable in my own skin I am destined to excel in all that I do.

I can work towards leading a life immune to status anxiety in a world where conformism is not only rife, but constant over-reliance on others for directions and 'lifestyle plagiarisms' clothed as 'inspiration' seems to be much more fashionable than uniqueness or the art of looking within for genuine answers.

Whilst I am not in denial that I come with my own unique brand of short-comings, I can remain firm in my conviction that my potential to reach whatever goals I set myself can, indeed, be limitless. As long as I am willing to dedicate the time and energy to the identification, exploration and the eventual connection with my inner resources, building the necessary hope, optimism and the courage to achieve any objective I set myself – including the seemingly impossible – would be but a matter of time.

And whilst I may sometimes consider myself to be 'lord' over certain territories in my life, which some people call 'expertise' – be it in my professional career or vocation – the notion of me being limited in other areas in terms of skill or know-how will not be a major cause for concern. My awareness of both my skills and knowledge deficits is a positive step because the born optimist within encourages me to regularly self-evaluate; removing my muddied lenses to capture the bigger picture. By so doing, not only would I be redefining what the outside world chooses to label 'weakness' as 'potential strength', but also exploring new pathways for my self-development, optimal performance and excellence in every facet of my life.

Rather than developing an inferiority complex by shying away from my inadequacies, I can learn to accept them for what they really are; there is nothing shameful about tripping and falling down a few times in any undertaking so long as staying down is never an option. And instead of dreading those, seemingly unavoidable, negative elements that life presents me, I can, with a genuine inner smile, accommodate them. For the same so-called elements that pose as barricades in my path to achievement, may just happen to be the recipes to success that I need to attain self-actualisation and for making a positive contribution to humankind.

My enhanced inner resource can enable me to defy the gravity of life's pessimism which, every now and again, threatens to pull me down. And deep within me lies that untapped resource that enables me to transform, what was once deemed an 'impossible mission', into a truly achievable aspiration.

Like one transient moment of darkness in my life that enables me to appreciate the faintest ray of sunlight, my shortcomings can, in the same vein, help me further appreciate the nature of my strengths. As another day on my journey draws closer to its inevitable end, the one invaluable lesson I have chosen to internalise is the notion that the less time I commit to trying to 'fix' my flaws the more there'll be for nurturing and growing my potential.

Day 47

Come rain, sunshine, sleet or snow, warmth or cold, life's raging storms will have no bearing on my positive mindset. I can create my very own favourable atmospheric weather conditions to take with me wherever I go.

My mind is the one true phenomenon with the capacity to create an environment of peace and calm, both within and around me, even in the most turbulent of mental and physical situations. For my mind is the fertile ground of my consciousness upon which whatever brand of thoughts I choose become planted and rooted to permeate every aspect of my life.

Whilst I am the product of my own thoughts, which translate into my decisions, actions and commensurate outcomes, I am also the creator of these same thoughts that have the propensity to transform what was once, for me, a virtual fantasy into a physical reality. Armed with the power to, in the same breath, create both destructive and life-enhancing thoughts perhaps it would be in my interest to make concerted efforts to choose the thoughts I generate carefully. For if my thoughts serve as the seeds from which my goals, dreams and aspirations all sprout and blossom into reality, then why not take personal responsibility for their nurture? Whilst I am under no illusion that life's storms can potentially stifle the growth of my mind's seeds, I can learn not to be mentally consumed by anxieties of drought brought about by a lack of rain or sunshine.

Taking personal responsibility for the growth of my seeds of success would mean paying little or no attention to the erratic nature of surrounding factors such as the weather, over which I have little, or no, control. Instead, I can channel my energy on areas that I truly know I am more than capable of influencing. And even if the growth and nurture of these seeds of success is entirely dependent on me finding a 'watering can' in the absence of rain, then so be it. Or should natural sunlight prove elusive when the seeds require the sun's rays to stimulate growth, I will not be moved; for like an adept and undeterred indoor gardener I will find the best artificial light source there is as substitute.

Thoughts that are detrimental to my well-being, growth, and development as an individual will be challenged; for I know that consciously planting the seeds of worry or nervousness on the mind's fertile grounds is an impediment to optimal human functioning. Negative mental states such as gloom, despondency, irascibility, grudges and hatred only serve to make me vulnerable and reactive to the slightest outward change or provocation.

Making a conscious decision to plant righteous thoughts on the fertile grounds of my mind feeds my subconscious with positive messages which, in turn, creates a commensurate physical environment. Needless to say, my external world situations and circumstances is a physical duplicate of the seeds I choose to sow in the mental realm. The thoughts and emotions I generate in the world within me is what I am bound to experience in the physical world around me.

Yes, I am aware that gaining full mastery of the workings of my mind is a journey of a lifetime that demands days, months and years of constant practice. And, yes, I am also aware that by evoking the spirit of the born optimist within me, I am continuously reminded that the word 'impossibility' will continue to mean nothing to me in my quest for success, as long I am prepared to dedicate each day to planting within me one positive seed at a time.

Today is the day I set out to become the architect of my mind's activities, for an uncontrolled mind is no different from a passenger aircraft's autopilot system; whilst it has been designed and developed to control its own engines, it would still require a great deal of human monitoring and intervention to avert a catastrophic crash.

Day 48

In my life there will be victorious days as well as days of defeat; regardless of the gravity of any setback, the mere fact that I am alive to experience and learn from such in itself represents my greatest victory of all.

Because I know that within me lie all the ingredients that make a true champion – a champion that can train himself to find some sort of meaning, or see an opportunity, in every adversity. A champion who is willing to accept even the most extreme of life's tragedies for what they are, and through post-traumatic growth, transform these tragedies into personal triumphs.

For me to assume the mantle of this champion of whom I speak, it is imperative that I learn one fundamental quality of all true champions: the willingness to understand that being a winner also means being able to exude grace and dignity in defeat like I would in victory. Likewise, learning to cultivate within me the foresight to view all setbacks as temporary phases, as opposed to final outcomes, would facilitate both my mental and spiritual growth.

The fact that no human being has ever been born with a 'loser' placard dangling around his or her neck, makes it all the more evident to me that my path through life is not predestined to be a certain way, hence, I remain thankful for the high degree of influence I am able to exercise over my own destiny. From my choice of thoughts, attitude, behaviour and decisions, right through to my vision, timescale and plan of action, I remain the overseer-in-chief of my personal outcomes. Regardless of the perception of having been born into, or raised in, an environment where the term 'bleak future' is prevalent, I can find solace in the knowledge that whom I choose to become will be solely determined by my inner decisions, and not the my surroundings or the limiting opinions of my doubters. Neither should the notion of being born into, or raised in, conditions that are inimical to the achievement of my personal goals become a career death sentence for me. Why? Because if there is one being who has the inner control and power to positively change the direction of his life, I need not look any further, for that very individual is the one who stares back at me when I gaze into the mirror.

There will, no doubt, be days when I find myself culpable for certain precarious situations; likewise, other days, when these situations may be caused by circumstances outside of my immediate influence or control. Be that as it may, to remain, or not to remain, in such situations and how I go about doing so will be my sole decision and no one else's.

My mind can be likened to a magnet; if I so will it, it is potent enough to attract the physical equivalent of whatever it is I decree to happen for myself in the mental realm. If I wake up to the thought of winning, and I visualise nothing but winning, I can reinforce the message by employing a daily routine of positive inner dialogues and conversations. By so doing, these 'success messages' become embedded in my subconscious, thereby increasing my chances of making them a reality as I begin to match each of my positive thoughts and emotions with a commensurate decision and action. Over time, my thoughts, decisions, behaviour and actions would have no choice but precipitate into my desired outcomes.

As for the men and women who perpetually carry bleak emotions within them, I have resolved to move as far away as I can from such company; for it is only a matter of time before pessimism discovers that gloom and despondency are its only companions.

Day 49

I can learn to always smile within my souls through both good and bad times. For one genuine inner smile within may be all it takes for prosperity and endless opportunities to present themselves.

When the tentacles of life's negative stress all seem to be overwhelmingly reaching out to me, becoming too much to bear, to whom do I turn? Do I face up to these perils; embracing them like just another undesirable means to a joyous end? Or do I stop dead in my tracks, refusing to proceed because I choose to perceive this particular barricade life has erected in my path to success as insurmountable? Perhaps I can occasionally pause, reflect and ask myself if, by any stretch of the imagination, I could possibly be in a worse situation than that which I am currently facing. Or, perhaps, I would do well to spare a thought for that individual somewhere in the world right now who would happily trade their perceived 'worse place' with my so-called 'bad place'? I choose to believe that, rather than lead a stagnated life, I am motivated to channel my energy and focus, day in, day out, into constantly evolving as a human being in every area of my life. By identifying and connecting with my inner resources, I know that I can stem the tide of pessimism that sometimes threatens to engulf my spirit. For I strongly attribute the realisation my goals, dreams and aspirations to learning to be at one with my core essence of self, which will, in turn, form the spiritual platform for all of my successes of the present and the future. From now, until the very end of my days, embracing the simplest of life's precious gifts will be the norm. For every new day I am fortunate to wake up and breathe the morning air should, in itself, represent a perfect gift from life worthy of my appreciation and celebration, irrespective of how negative my appraisal of my life's circumstances may seem at that very moment.

Each morning I feel the force of my inner motivation drive me out from the lazy comfort of my bed, is a day I can do well to remember that it isn't what, or where, I currently am in my life that spurred me into getting out of that bed but, instead, what I aspire to be or refuse to become. For what chance do I stand in changing an undesirable status quo if am deprived of the wonderful gift of life. If cemeteries are filled with the corpses of many an individual whose unfulfilled dreams were buried with them, who am I not to make the most of every opportunity whilst I still have the gift of life at my disposal?

I know that I am, most definitely not, a hundred per cent immune from the odd disappointment, dejection, or dashed hope, arising from my often lofty expectations of myself, others and life in general. I also know that I have what it takes to soften the emotional impact of disappointment by practicing the art of being at inner peace with myself. For it is this equanimity within my soul that reminds me that, even though everything that surrounds me has the propensity to change from time to time – from the behaviours and characters of people I'm in contact with on a day-to-day basis, to situations and events – I can learn to remain centred and unperturbed. I can also practice improving my well-being; enhancing both my performance and motivation levels, by instilling within me the notion of not trying to control the activities of others, but rather influencing them by focusing on improving my own outlook on life.

Day 50

Whilst there are bound to be tragic occurrences in the course of my life, what defines me won't be the occurrence of these tragic events in themselves but the attitude I choose to adopt in response to the tragedies in question.

I can learn that my initial emotional response of choice to the situations or events I deem as unpleasant is what sets the tone for my overall approach to tackling those challenges.

Taking the time to tune my mental lenses into taking another look at the so-called 'bad news' may reveal to me that the situation in question may not be as intrinsically 'bad' as I first envisaged, but merely an image I've unwittingly granted my mind permission to project. If my mental portrayal of setbacks – both minor and major – is constantly that of catastrophe or failure there is a propensity for this style of thinking to impede my drive and motivation; transforming my quest for success from what was once an image of possibility into nothing more than a mirage-like entity.

I can prevent the negativity of my emotions – borne out of life's adverse elements – from knocking me back, by setting my sights on a future filled with opportunities. And if I so will it, hope and optimism can become the engine room of my inner motivation vehicle which, itself, is driven by courage and enables me to overcome life's challenging spells – especially those critical moments when I feel like I'm running on 'empty'. And because I know my inner vision of 'bright lights' can become an emblem of my future aspirations, I will never lose sight of reaching my very own 'promised land'. For my 'bright lights' have the power to infinitely shine upon me in all that I do, eclipsing the shadows of life's despondent darkness which looms in times of extreme difficulty and hardship.

I am also of the firm conviction that there lies an element of beauty in the art of relentlessly striving to move upwards even when the world around me is on a downward spiral. With this in mind, I will consciously continue to gravitate towards this wondrous horizon ahead of me owing to what I see as the powers it possesses in aligning my current reality with my future aspirations, one day at a time.

As the sun sets to mark the end of yet another fruitful day in my life, I feel instilled with a sense of renewed purpose, drive and energy; and, more significantly, a stronger belief that the things my heart and mind conceive are, more likely than not, the very things the sweat of my hands will achieve.

And in terms of setbacks; whilst the past, as I know it, is unchangeable my future remains filled with promise. With today's inner resolve I aim to begin shaping the direction of my tomorrow with not just the quality of the thoughts I generate today, but also the effort I put in.

Day 51

Not only will this day see me rid myself of my rags of doom, despondency and despair, I will also endeavour to adorn my life with the beautiful garments of positivity.

Today is the day I work towards leaving no room for the negative emotions of anxiety and trepidation. For a life tainted with both is one that is perpetually subservient to fate and circumstances as against being in control of its own destiny. I can also learn to become a master of my emotions, rather than a slave to them; for a life ruled by emotions alone is a life dictated to by rash decisions and ill-advised actions, a bit like sprinting through life trying to avoid land mines.

If I begin to take personal responsibility for my thoughts, and how I use the limitless inner resources at my mind's disposal, I will find that the art of creating thoughts of inner bliss and happiness which often prove challenging at the start, with regular mental practice, can become second nature to me. And because I know I am more likely to engage in success behaviours if, within my mind, I make a series of arguments in favour of that very change I'd like to see materialise in my life, I will continue to employ the use of positive self talk on a day-to-day basis. By constantly describing what I want and how I want it to be – even if I don't yet know how to achieve a particular goal – I am sowing seeds of self-belief in the fertile grounds of my mind that will eventually align my thoughts with activities that lead to the actualisation of those visions.

And it won't really matter how long it takes me to get there for I have, slowly but surely, begun to imbibe the culture of the born optimist, which is to perceive success in its entirety not just as a destination, but a journey of a lifetime. For I am embracing a philosophy that will remind me every single time that just because my determination to succeed is sometimes slowed down by adversity, doesn't equate to it being stopped altogether. And just because I sometimes find myself being held down by obstacles, doesn't mean that I am completely halted in my tracks. The mere fact that the successful outcomes I aim for in certain areas of my life are subject to delays, doesn't necessarily mean I will ultimately be denied my desired goals.

Today is the day I see myself climbing down from the fence of futile fears I have, for many a year, sat on complacently. A day I dust off the remainder of life's cobwebs and usher in a new era of mental 'spring-cleaning' which will ultimately result in the positive transformations I seek.

As today draws to its fruitful end let me, once again, use this precious moment to remind myself that I owe it to myself, and no one else, to find and fulfil my personal calling in life through the use of the only reliable means available to me: my inner motivation.

Day 52

The unsavoury lessons of my life's setbacks can be balanced with savouring the sweet scent of its successes.

I am prepared to accept that, in order for me to fully embrace the euphoric feeling that comes with accomplishment of any sort, it is imperative for me to have experienced the sour side of the spectrum.

For instance, the beauty of being healthy and physically mobile can only be truly appreciated if I've experienced the pain of incapacity that ill-health can bring. This, in itself, reinforces to me how my appreciation of the term 'being healthy', which I often take for granted, would take on a whole new meaning if I found myself bedridden with an illness of whatever kind. Likewise, the presence of everything and anything I term as 'good' in my life is only accentuated and made more relevant by the conspicuous absence of that very thing in my life. Success, in the same vein, is perhaps a concept I can learn to appreciate better once I've had a fundamental understanding of the traits of its nemesis – the lack of it.

The born optimist within me has, today, reinforced the message that, provided I dedicate the time and effort to relentlessly honing my craft, I can become successful on an unimaginable scale. That said, I am all too aware that the true test of my character won't be measured against the good times alone, but also the stoic attitude I exhibit in times of adversity – those dark periods in my life when all of my accomplishments appear as nothing more than distant memories. And when those dark clouds do arrive, hovering ominously above my head, threatening to blow away my dreams in their infancy, whom or to what do I turn? Do I simply give in, retiring permanently from the race track of life? Or, to the contrary, do I relax, reflect and attempt to find a meaning and an opportunity within each of my struggles, for my own spiritual growth and personal development.

And when I eventually achieve that success I've worked all my life to attain, I will not stop there; for the true essence of success isn't just about having it but, more importantly, retaining it, building on it and using it to positively impact the lives of others. I view success as a paradoxical phenomenon which, with hard work, careful planning and determination, anyone can attain but, at the same time, very few can sustain. Hence my need to experience the unpleasant phase of being without it in order to be mentally prepared to not only reach for it, but also strive to sustain and enhance its value once it's finally within my grasp.

Were success to be a newborn I would be its nurturing mother; mentally assuming the character of a woman who either gave birth to her only child (called success) quite late in her life; or a 'mother' who has had to suffer the psychological pain of being previously medically pronounced as being 'unable to conceive'. Adopting this perspective on success can spur me on in ensuring I pay great care and due diligence in the handling of each and every one of my accomplishments – be they great or small.

Day 53

Behind every victory is a formula for its attainment; perhaps the best time to consider changing my winning formula is the day that winning formula stops winning.

Is there really a point to desperately seeking new answers to old problems when the old way of doing things has proven to be just as good – if not better?

Is it not conceivable that each and every progressive step I've taken in my life came with a certain way of doing things which got me to my desired outcome? That said, it is important that I don't become allergic to change as there will be instances where being complacently trapped in the status quo could be detrimental to my growth and personal development. And just because one way of doing things worked for me in certain circumstances does not necessarily make it a tested and trusted formula for tackling a brand new challenge.

Perhaps learning to be adaptive to life's changes – absolute or transitional – is the key to being successful in my personal pursuits. My ability to strike the right balance between the appropriate time to switch gears (adaptability), and when to simply stick to what worked in days gone by, is an art surely worth perfecting in my approach to everyday challenges.

There will no doubt be days when – perhaps owing to things not going my way – I find myself experiencing self-doubt and, what can only be described as, a 'conviction deficit syndrome' of some sort. And when that day comes, rather than panic or falter, I will strive to find meaning in that particular self-generated doubt – what it represents for me, how logical it is and, more importantly, how to counteract it in the most balanced and constructive of ways.

Being cautiously realistic in my approach does not, and will never, equate to being petrified of a challenge in my personal success lexicon. Instead, observing such precautions prior to making final decisions would, for me, be symptomatic of learning to think things through; weighing the pros and cons before embarking on those life-changing decisions.

Day 54

Today marks the dawn of a new era; an era where I find myself transformed from the driven to the driver in the affairs of my own life.

Whilst I may not have the power or ability to control how people think, what they say and how they choose to conduct themselves, I am more than capable of influencing those around me by being exemplary in how I behave and communicate my thoughts and ideas.

Rather than settling for the role of a mere spectator who would rather watch events unfold, I can do one better and become both a driver and participant in the process of positive change. And not only will I constantly seek out avenues for self-improvement, I will also be committed to devising new ways of being a source of hope to the hopeless and an inspiration to those living uninspired lives. So, bidding farewell to the reactive type of human existence where I find myself simply responding to events I once deemed as 'outside forces', perhaps the time has come for me to become more proactive in how I deal with challenging situations.

And, yes, there will be many a situation where I am faced with both the unchangeable and immovable elements of life for which I am neither responsible, nor in control of, not to mention occasions where I'll find myself between the proverbial rock and a hard place without the slightest ray of hope or optimism.

Through it all, I will strive to stand firm and not be moved by each of these adverse events – for those things I cannot change, adapt, or avoid altogether, I will learn to focus on finding meaning, experience and wisdom within them. For I see the art of learning to create and influence my life's realities and outcomes as a lifelong pursuit in itself which aligns to my core values. Why wait for the wind of change to blow me in whichever direction it so chooses when the born optimist within encourages me to create my own unique path to follow?

As long as my focus on my aspiration remains relentless and is matched with an appropriate plan of action for its accomplishment, the term 'failure' will surely be the least of my concerns.

Day 55

As my resolve to never give in strengthens with each passing minute, my lofty ambitions of reaching the summit of success begins to manifest with each passing day.

If being relentlessly focused is my vehicle of choice in the attainment of success, constancy of purpose will be the fuel that runs the engine of that vehicle. I can either continue to strive towards fulfilling my potential each passing day or be content to watch myself slowly slip into procrastination and inertia. And because I've chosen to act rather than wait for something to happen, the desired changes I seek will ultimately become manifest in every area of my life.

Depending on how I choose to perceive it, a life once tainted with hardship can be transformed into that of a beautiful struggle. And just because my desired outcomes and results don't manifest instantly, despite my best efforts, does not mean that much sought after 'light at the end of a dark tunnel' in my human existence won't ultimately reveal itself.

Provided I continue to tread on the path of self-nurture conjoined with altruism, I'll eventually be united with that very light of success which I seek and whether it finds me, or I discover it first, will be immaterial. Because I have learnt that most success stories are born on the back of visionaries rising to act where procrastinators chose to slumber, I will never give up or give in to adversity or complacency. And if I borrow ideas from the men and women who have usurped the positions of individuals who chose to hang up their boots instead of persisting, I will do just fine.

I will never trivialise the virtues and rewards that come with constancy of purpose, for history books are littered with stories of many individuals whose lives have been transformed from the abyss of obscurity to the echelons of prosperity. This day I begin my march towards tomorrow and beyond, hopeful and optimistic that my willingness to adopt the right kind of attitude will, each passing day, gravitate me closer to my goals.

Day 56

Rather than be content with being a mere anticipator of positive change I can become its initiator.

For as long as I possess a will, backed by the determination to succeed, a way will never cease to exist. If I am willing to put in the time and effort in conjunction with my vision I can become that ordinary man possessing the innovative mind to achieve extraordinary feats.

The dawn of yet another day comes with an inner resolve to become an initiator of change rather than its anticipator. And through this steely resolve, coupled with planting one seed of change at a time, in my heart I can achieve 'something' out of the very thing that was once deemed as 'nothing' in my life.

From the furnace of my struggles, I will forge a protective armour to counteract the intrusive thoughts in my head that seek to derail me from fulfilling my life's purpose. For it is at this very point that the born optimist within once again intervenes by reassuring me that it is okay – and human – to experience negative thoughts and feelings once in a while, so long as I don't confuse those self-limiting emotions with rational ones.

Today signals the beginning of a new era where I begin to take personal responsibility for the endeavours I set out to achieve by consistently seeing them through to their logical end. More significantly, I will seek to unearth the motivational reasons behind the need to excel in every undertaking I choose to commit to. And whilst I acknowledge that motivation itself remains the vehicle that transports me from the place I am now to where I aspire to be, my personal motivational reasons provide the fuel that powers the engine of that very vehicle.

I know, that with the right focus and dedication to the cause, I can become a true visionary, leader and an ambassador for change in my own right whatever adverse conditions I find myself in. And other than catering to the needs of my soul I will also aspire towards being self-transcendental and altruistic in all of my dealings and interactions with my fellow men and women. For the consequences and effects of sharing the love and kindness of my heart with other human beings through the virtuous work of my hands can be likened to the effects of the sun. Benevolent and indiscriminate in its characteristics, the sun shines on every region of the globe; brightening up the faces of multitudes and touching the lives of millions without being discriminatory, prejudicial or in any way hateful.

I will also do well to constantly remind myself, when faced with today and tomorrow's challenges, that nothing will be too difficult for me to achieve provided I am prepared to rise from my couch of complacency to become the vehicle and driver for change rather than one of its many passengers.

Day 57

To build hope, and enhance my optimism, I will continue to acknowledge and internalise my past and present accomplishments. For sustained self-motivation not only hinges on my ability to comfortably recall and relive what I've done well in my life, but the things I continue to do very well.

There will be days when, try as I might, I find myself struggling to understand my motivational reason behind the pursuit of a particular goal or in my performance of certain tasks. There will be times when my motivational reason is encrusted with layers and layers of negative stress in the form of setbacks, disappointments, the pessimism of others, interpersonal conflicts and, what I perceive to be, life's overwhelming demands on my everyday existence.

Come that moment when my life's circumstances seem to approach me with a hurricane-like velocity, I will pause for a minute and reflect on those things that have gone according to plan in my life. For every one major disappointment I encounter I can look within and tap into my reservoir of 'success memories' to counteract each negative experience with at least two or three positive memories.

I can learn to understand that, when it comes to the power of inner motivation, not even the so-called 'bad memory' can come between me and my ability to consciously recall my past accomplishments. And, contrary to popular belief, I can dare to believe that there is no such thing as a 'good' or 'bad' memory; my subjective view of what's 'good' or 'bad' lies in the nature of my ability to recall stored information of positive experiences when I really need them to stave off negative emotions. With this in mind, not only will I continue to draw strength from the memories of my past achievements, I will also tune into the specific success behaviours which led to those achievements in the first place.

Whilst modesty may be a virtuous thing, I may also do well to understand that there is a fine line between modesty and knocking my own self-esteem. Hence, when I am paid a genuine compliment by others for what is definitely as a result of my hard work, not only will I accept and acknowledge the praise, I will also make it a point of duty to internalise it. For my mind is akin to a seed requiring constant nurture through self-praise or that which comes from others when deserved; to starve it of this is to stifle my own personal development and growth which are crucial to achieving my goals, dreams and aspirations.

Whilst modesty is essential for keeping me grounded, my ability to recall, relive and replicate a 'success memory' will equip me with the much-needed self-motivation techniques and strategies required to break down the countless obstacles which stand between me and the realisation of my dreams.

Day 58

The first step forward on my journey towards positive change lies in my refusal to accept the status quo.

My journey towards change not only begins with my desire for self-improvement but also dissatisfaction with certain elements of my current situation. Whilst my motivational reasons for wanting these personal changes in my situation to take effect are rooted in my strong desire for benefit, I will never discount the need to avoid negative consequences. Whatever the motivational reasons for doing the things I get out of bed to do on a day-to-day basis, it is of the utmost importance that my actions align with my core values. Otherwise, I will be plagued by inner conflict leading to a crisis of identity and a life devoid of purpose.

This morning will be the first of many that will see me begin to explore, identify and connect with my inner resources. I will also aim to use this opportunity to cultivate my very own pathway to lateral and divergent thinking – key assets that would ensure I stop applying outdated solutions to new problems.

Similarly, today will be the first of many where I consciously turn my back on, what I see as, 'popular conformism' – a trend borne out of the pressure to mimic what is regarded as a socially endorsed pattern of thinking, speaking or behaving for fear of public ridicule. And because I firmly believe that being true to myself and being 'authentic' trumps the concept of popularity every time, I will think, act and speak in a manner that is not only true to me but also conforms with my core values.

If I feel there is a certain change needed – and that I feel strongly about – to positively impact my life and those of others in my immediate community and the society at large, why look over my shoulder to see what others may or may not do before I feel compelled to act? Considering that the born optimist within me reminds me of how innovators make things happen, whilst procrastinators tend to watch things happen, should there still be any argument in favour of inaction on my part?

Day 59

Before life's adversities tempt me to utter the words 'I give in', the hope and optimism inside of me will respond with the message 'stand firm and persevere for your victory is near'.

For every negative thought, emotional upheaval or obstacle that threatens to instil self-limiting beliefs within me, there exists a positive mental assertion and a 'success memory' to neutralise it.

For within me lies an unwavering sense of hope and an optimistic spirit, that constantly reassures me that, regardless of the magnitude of the difficulties confronting me, I am bound to make it to the very end. As for the so-called 'mission challenging' elements in my life: so long as I'm committed to facing them head on they will never become 'mission impossible'.

To achieve the level of success that I crave, it is imperative for me to understand that self-motivation is, in itself, an art; and rather than be viewed as something which occurs by accident, it should be perceived as a phenomenon which can manifest purely by my own design. In order to successfully tap into it, by fully utilising my inner resources, it will take a certain level of insight, reflection and objective self-evaluation: knowing who I am, what I am capable of, what I've been through and, ultimately, what I aspire to be. For it is only by being attuned to my inner resources and my very own personalised emotional significance for wanting to succeed in life that I'd be empowered to make that successful transition from what was once a 'stillborn potential' to bringing to life that very potential.

It will also take a certain kind of hunger and drive within me to create the vision and imagery upon which my pathways to success will be hinged. The act of creating mere visions and pathways, however, would both be meaningless endeavours if I am averse to engaging in the day-to-day mental rehearsals required to transform these slowly evolving visions into fast-paced realities. For I am of the firm conviction that engaging in regular positive inner conversations and the daily habit of documenting each thought and feeling in the form of this diary, can indeed yield positive dividends.

I will also learn to cultivate within me a self-motivation culture of mental performance simulation – a process where I project desired images of not just what I aim to do to reach my goals, or how; but more importantly what I will be doing when I have accomplished those goals, even if a part of me remains deeply pessimistic about the reality of success. Whilst I can understand the efficacy of beginning projects with an end in mind, I will also embrace the concept of moment-to-moment awareness that is required in putting smaller goals together to reach larger objectives. If my ultimate goal was a final picture or image, the moment by moment process would be the pixels that make up that final picture.

In a world of the expected, it's a given that, in order to be successful in certain areas of human endeavour, I need to work on my 'aptitude'; in the realm of the unexpected, however, I can only adapt to my new realities through attitude, not just aptitude. Attitude will serve as my medication of choice to soothe away the pains and aches that accompany the setbacks I encounter along the way on my path to success. For it will, indeed, take some degree of stoicism on my part, plus a steely nerve, resilience and doggedness to remain standing head and shoulders above my self-limiting trepidations in order to prevail.

This is the day I will begin to rid my life of the various emotional diseases constantly eating away my cloak of confidence. For this day, like many more days to come after it, will see me welcome beauty into my life by adorning my inner world with renewed hope and a sense of optimism as I walk the golden path to prosperity – a path that is only walked along by true born optimists.

Day 60

I know exactly where my talents and creativity lie, for it is mainly in this direction I aim to fly.

Today calls for embracing the possibility that as long as I commit myself to exploring, identifying and connecting with my own unique strengths and inner resources on a day-to-day basis, attaining success in every area of my life will be but a matter of time. Be it in education, creativity, business, science, humanitarian work or family life; I will strive to identify and connect with my inherent forte – one which I know I'm probably better at delivering compared to anyone else. As challenging a task as this may sometimes seem, one thing is certain; until my goals and life pursuits all align with my personal calling the words 'well-being', 'success' and 'happiness' will be but a figment of my imagination. Not only will I seek to nurture and develop my potential, unique talents and creativity I will also strive to channel all my positive energy towards altruistic outcomes.

From this day forth, I will cease to expend precious moments and energy ruminating over my past failings and shortcomings when such energy can be better served in harnessing my strengths to their fullest potential.

Today is a day that will see my overall perspective of the outer world becoming a journey predominantly shaped by the inner workings of my mind. For I believe within my heart and mind that a self-examined life is the gateway to self-discovery; a journey which would, in turn, bridge the gap between my life's present realities and its future possibilities. Plus, learning to focus inwardly for solutions will broaden my horizons with regards to the countless possibilities at my disposal on the road to being a driver for positive change and not just a passenger in the change process.

Day 61

My aiming high in life to reach the pinnacle of success requires not just an intellectual aptitude but also a right mental attitude; a world filled with education and expertise but devoid of self-motivation only creates a regressive society and never a progressive one.

Possessing the right amount of technical skill and know-how in any undertaking is one thing, but it is quite another having the inner motivation and right frame of mind for its execution. The fine line between my accomplishments and setbacks will, more often than not, be dependent on how I choose to apply the inner workings of my mind and not necessarily the tools I have at my disposal.

And whilst the right mental attitude can induce positive performances, a negative one is vulnerable to shoddy and poor quality work in every area of my human endeavours.

Hence, if I resolve, today, to give the very best of me in all that I do in terms of my performance levels, I will, more frequently, attract the kind of results I am aiming for. And even when my desired outcomes aren't so forthcoming, the born optimist inside of me will never cease reassuring me that it is always possible to excel in any undertaking, provided I persist and continue to find a positive meaning and opportunity to learn and grow within every adversity. And I will hold on to the belief that I can always adapt to my life's ever-changing realities regardless of what adversities are thrown at me.

My journey in this direction begins with the creation of happy thoughts; the calibre of thoughts and emotions that bring about a genuine inner smile; a brand of inner peace which paves the way for self-belief and courage in the eye of any of life's brewing storms. From within me will I also generate a 'stay-good' factor (not just the transitory 'feel-good' experience) to serve as a constant reminder that, provided I am prepared to adjust my way of thinking, I can spot golden opportunities even when clothed in layer upon layer of trials and tribulations.

I know it can be done, and I am positive it will be done. And this won't be tomorrow, next week or next year; for the right approach and mental attitude to all things present and future begins NOW. For I have thrown off my complacent attitude with one aim and one aim only: to create my very own positive imagery of success and transform it from what was once a mere vision to its corresponding reality.

Day 62

My genuine happiness and inner peace will be built upon approaching life's ever changing conditions – good and bad – with one mind and spirit; neither being too elated by my life's successes nor deflated by its setbacks.

Today is the day I seek to inculcate within me the art of calm and balance in my conduct, behaviours, and overall demeanour. For the approach I adopt in dealing with life's events, to a great degree, will determine my eventual outcomes and plays a significant factor in my self-motivation and overall well-being. Based on this premise, I will wrap my mind in a cloak of calm reflection to contemplate life's numerous complexities and appreciate its simplicities.

By subjecting my conduct to the dictates of inner calm in relation to my relationships with the others, I will remain loving, affectionate and charitable to my fellow men and women. And this responsibility to self and others won't be hinged upon the vagaries of the weather – as it won't matter whether the sun shines on me or if all I see are dark clouds hovering above my head. Whilst altruism reminds me of my moral obligation and responsibility to the wider world around me, being at one with my very own core essence in all that I think, say, or do, equips me with both the social and emotional intelligence to engage appropriately with others whether or not they hold similar or contrasting views and values to mine.

Learning to become of one mind and spirit not only makes me assertive and stronger mentally, it also helps me to build both the durable inner resources and the necessary coping mechanisms to stave off negative stress brought about by life's sometimes overwhelming challenges.

This very day, I will find myself transformed to a more controlled being; one who has opted to bid a final farewell to reactive ways and, in its stead, imbibe a more proactive personal culture. The day I feel myself having a higher degree of influence over my world coupled with the belief that, with the right actions, I can contribute positively to the larger world around me – one deed at a time.

Whilst setting out in the quest to succeed on yet another glorious day, let me take one brief moment to pause and reflect over today's motivational pill for my soul's healing: am I complacent with being a rudderless boat aimlessly ploughing through the sea of life? Or, to the contrary, I can assume the role of the assured captain who not only possesses great knowledge of his vessel but has – with experience – mastered the art of navigating his vessel safely through the harshest of life's tempests That decision, as ever, will inevitably be mine and no one else's.

Day 63

Whilst every constructive criticism levelled at me is no more than an inspirational vehicle for change, the destructive ones can only serve as my motivational platform for persistence and continuity.

Today I am going to take stock of the complex feelings of discomfort I tend to struggle with when it comes to the things others say, think and do in relation to me.

Rather than becoming too consumed with, what I may perceive as, the negativity of others towards me I can channel my energy and focus into my own reactions and attitude. For when it comes to the occasional landmine nature of public perception, the opinions of others and interpersonal relationships in general, the attitude I choose to exhibit is all I can control. With this in mind, I will work on paying closer attention to my interpretation of what is said, or implied, by others, with the intention of challenging those personal beliefs that I find damaging to my well-being, growth and personal development, whilst retaining the balanced and constructive ones. For I need to realise that it isn't really what people say about me that is the most significant source of my negative stress, but my personal understanding and interpretation of those views and opinions others have about me.

Now that I am conscious that I possess more power and control over how I process the information I receive than what is actually said or implied in the court of public opinion, I can work towards using my energy and control to counteract any negative perspective on what I personally deem as unduly critical comments.

Likewise, I can learn to relive such setbacks and rewrite certain aspects of events that do not conform to the new positive attitude I have chosen to adopt going forward. An attitude which empowers me with the humility to accept all things constructive and the strength of character to adapt to the realities of the destructive ones; or better still, to rise above such negativity.

For me to become that 'authentic' being who refuses to be enslaved by public opinion, perhaps borrowing a leaf from the book of those who have been before me would be a step in the right direction – those great men and women who happen to be the true embodiment of humility bound with self-belief. I can strive towards replicating their approach which demanded they narrow the focus of their energy to enhancing their actual strengths, whilst also dedicating each and every minute of their day to working on improving their potential strengths.

I can aspire to being exemplary when it comes to exuding a sense of magnanimity in my personal victories and setbacks. Irrespective of how successful I may become now or, in the future, I will still consult with 'mentors' for guidance from time to time; open-mindedly accepting guidance and direction from those who have been there and done it. And, in the case of the men and women I am in direct contact with on a day-to-day basis who see fit to – justifiably or otherwise – critique my every conduct, I will learn to heed their genuine criticisms; taking the superlative praise with the negative. That said, I will also accept what is, arguably, the gospel truth that not all criticism I receive is necessarily intended to improve me as a person or the quality of my work; there will always be the kind that comes with an element of malicious intent. So rather than getting knocked off my perch or being trapped in a web of animosity and counter-animosity, my righteous path of choice will be to stand firm and utilise the negativity for the purpose of enhancing my performance and productivity.

From this day forth, the born optimist within me has chosen to perceive my personal success as not something that will be determined by what I am able to prove to the world, but what I am able to prove to myself.

Day 64

Not achieving success yesterday or today will not prevent me from attaining my desired outcomes tomorrow.

Success, as I choose to perceive it, won't stop at the positive outcomes of my efforts alone for the attitude I exude in relation to each of my setbacks will also be a major contributing factor.

I can either adopt an attitude of resignation which brings with it a defeatist tone of finality in the handling of setbacks, or, to the contrary, I can choose to follow a path of hope, optimism and courage to achieve the seemingly impossible.

So long as I continue to engage my mind with positive inner conversations I remain strengthened in the knowledge that just because my success is not immediate, it doesn't mean it will never come. And because I've chosen to see hardships and difficulties as phases, rather than permanent states, I will be much more open to accepting negative results as mere knock-backs than outright failures. The fact that my dreams and aspirations sometimes appear to take an eternity to materialise is not proof that they will never ever come to fruition.

For the nature of the attitude I choose to adopt when faced with life's, often curve-ball-like, challenges is what transforms my aspirations from a mere spark of hope into a burning flame of optimism, spurring me on to greater things.

The positive attitude I choose to exhibit today will be akin to a flame that burns so bright within that it lights up the pathways to the realisation of every one of those aspirations. I can also learn to understand that, whilst embracing a new positive mode of thought in my darkest hour can make all the things I set out to achieve become possible, a negative heart and mind, on the other hand, merely stagnates my progress before that very journey of progress commences.

Day 65

I am my very own prototype; the qualities, abilities and potential that I possess are unique to me and me alone.

Regardless of what rung of social and economic ladder I may perceive myself, or others around me, as occupying, I will remain focused on the task ahead of me. Irrespective of how far ahead of me others are, or portray themselves as being, my mindset from now until infinity will be not to lose sight of where I am at the moment, whilst striving to reach the place I aim to be.

So long as I continue to remind myself that not only am I unique in my DNA, but also in my orientation, life experiences, talents and abilities, I will be just fine. To compare an apple's features with that of an orange – regardless of the fact that both are 'fruits' – is somewhat akin to counter intuitively comparing my life's purpose (and how I aim to fulfil it) to that of the next man or woman, simply because we're all classed as human beings. Inasmuch as we all share the same physical features we remain distinctly unique in our experiences, motivation and aspirations.

And simply because a particular type of career choice, car, house, faith, religion, sexual orientation or lifestyle in general suits my neighbour, friend, work colleague, or even family member, does not automatically guarantee the same would apply to me. Whilst the qualities I possess may differ slightly – or a great deal – when compared with those of other men and women, within these same differing qualities lies the potential for me to realise my goals, just like the next person – albeit through different paths.

159

From this day onwards, I will make a conscious decision to avoid the distractions of the world by turning my back on the cattle-like nature of 'following the Joneses'. Contrary to popular belief, I believe that age-old notion of 'strength' being inherent in 'numbers' may not necessarily be valid all the time. Likewise, the concept of 'popularity' does not always equate to 'authenticity' as the habit of working according to other people's agendas, at the expense of my own, can be inimical to my values, dignity, self-esteem and personal development.

As I declare myself 'lord' over my life, today, tomorrow and always, I will narrow my focus and energy to the pursuit of the things I have subjectively labelled as 'success ventures' and 'sources of happiness'. For I believe that not only is the word 'success' dependent on an individual's subjective definition, it is as diverse as the ethnicity of planet Earth's inhabitants never mind the number of languages being spoken within it.

From now into the future, the priority for me will be to keep working on making my own unique visions a reality, and paying minimal attention to fads or trends that are here one minute and nowhere to be found the next. After all, the success track of life is filled with those who conquer marathons and the ones who dominate sprints – none is less important than the other so long as they all successfully reach their respective goals.

Day 66

The one true hero I can call upon when surrounded by life's numerous adversities is none other than the dormant giant within me waiting patiently to be awoken.

As I open my eyes this morning to another day on my journey, in my continued resolve to seek inner solutions to external problems I've come to the realisation that if there exists one element in my life that I can gain more mastery and control over, above everything else, it is my mind. From the nature of thoughts generated within the corridors of my mind, to my words, deeds and behaviour, it is worthwhile remembering that the thoughts I create today, when verbalised through words, can become the cornerstone of tomorrow's outcomes. Even though there will be days I let myself and others down with irrational behaviour, I will restrain myself from being too self-critical, for personal change is a journey of a lifetime and never a final destination; a process I aim to embrace as that of pro-gression and never perfection. In terms of the direction which my life will take, I alone, and no one else, wields the power to transform my day-to-day assertions and utterances into self-fulfilling prophecies.

My ideas, potential, talent and creativity are like 'sleeping gi-ants' within me awaiting their respective cues to rise and propel my life to the pinnacle of greatness that it so rightly deserves. My body's sometimes slothful tendency to endorse the perpet-ual slumbering of these 'giants' within me can give rise to dwarf-like ambitions which should never be an option if I aim to maximise all of my potential to become the best I can be. When my mind is poverty-conscious, it will, like a magnet, pull everything associated with penury to its core; similarly, when it

161

is prosperity-conscious, the affluence and abundance it perceives is what it will consequently attracts.

Today, like previous days, will see me striving towards identifying and connecting with the inner strengths and resources I need to help me achieve my set goals. A day I celebrate life, living and the resurrection of the inner giant within me. A day I become re-energised to board that vehicle of inner motivation that can transport me from life's current realities to what I perceive as the fulfilment of its potential. Greatness will always be within my sight as long as I remain awake mentally, keeping vigilant in readiness to embrace it when it comes along.

With a renewed sense of hope, optimism and the courage to pursue my dreams rigorously, the term 'success', for me, will represent that journey made up of different phases and pit stops of personal setbacks and achievements rather than one singular destination.

Day 67

I have chosen knowledge and enlightenment as the guiding lights which illuminate the darkest of pathways both within and without; I owe it to me and no one else to continuously seek them out from wherever they may be.

I will embrace knowledge and enlightenment as the two paramount guiding philosophies with regards to my human existence and progress. How can I truly free myself from the tentacles of ignorance by ignoring the path leading to enlightenment?

If I ever find myself sinking neck-deep in a quicksand of ignorance, knowledge and enlightenment would represent the outstretched shrubs I reach out to for survival and intellectual resuscitation. I can become a firm believer in the act of rising from my comfort zone for the purpose of navigating beyond the restrictive borders of my mind. For it is only when my mind is nourished that I can successfully seek out the necessary information I lack to enhance the quality of my life and help to make the world in which I live a better place. And the more open I am to taking in new concepts and cultivating within me new ideas, the more equipped I'll be in coping with, and overcoming, the myriad of obstacles erected in my path to prevent me from fulfilling my life's purpose. Besides, the more I learn, the more I will begin to understand how my anxieties, insecurity and consequent disappointments tend to emanate from uncertainty which, in itself, is an offspring of ignorance.

In a world littered with minefields of wrong choices and ill-informed decisions, knowledge and enlightenment will be my trusted comrades – for knowledge and enlightenment are, to my mind, what a guide dog and a walking stick are to the blind. Not only would ushering them into my life keep my mind immune to self-limiting notions, but also instil within me the confidence and self-belief I need to rise above the cynicism of others. And because my self-esteem will become profoundly enhanced, I will begin to exude a more positive outlook of myself – a habit which would influence the way others see me.

As yet another day of soul-enriching inner conversation draws to an end, I am making a personal resolution that in every sphere of my life – be it in the arts or literary appreciation; business, religion, cultural or political, and in all my social and interpersonal relationships – there will only be one thing worth striving for: being in the know.

Day 68

As long as I'm still breathing, achieving anything and everything I set my heart and my mind to will be far from impossible.

I will begin today by ensuring my raw sentiments and emotions do not becloud my rationale and inner calm even in the face of the most trying of times.

As long as I continue to remind myself that there is always somewhere worse than the so-called 'bad place' in my experiences of adversity I will be just fine. And so long as I can recall, relive and re-enact the very things that I did right in the past, I can be optimistic that replicating my previous successes today and tomorrow is achievable.

I can learn from, and reflect upon, the stories of wealthy but terminally-ill men and women living on borrowed time; the ones who can afford everything else they desire but the one thing they crave the most; good health. And if my doubts and pessimism over the direction of my life remains unruffled I can perhaps spare a thought for the thousands of unfulfilled dreams trapped in corpses at various cemeteries around the world - the dead and buried men, women and children who, perhaps, would have given anything and everything to have another go at life.

With this in mind, perhaps the time has come for me to begin to appreciate every single moment of being alive with a renewed vigour and sense of conviction that no matter what direction life's numerous curve balls come at me, within me lies the inner resources to prevail. For I will embrace the kind of hope and optimism that isn't hinged on positive outcomes alone; even if my outcomes aren't the ones I desire I believe I possess the stoicism to endure, adapt and make the most of my life's new realities.

As I open my eyes to bear witness to the dawn of this new day I will celebrate the artistry and grandeur of Mother Nature's good work by taking in the warm breeze and freshness of the early morning air. Learning to occasionally divorce myself completely from life's hectic schedules, to focus on three or four things that I am thankful for each day, would continue to fuel my inner motivation vehicle and also help to stave off despondent feelings which, if left unchecked, can negatively impact my well-being and personal growth.

Day 69

A life devoid of dreams would probably be more worthwhile to me than one filled with many a dream but devoid of the self-belief, courage and passion to pursue those dreams.

In order to continue to build on, and sustain, my motivation levels I can draw strength and inspiration from the areas of my life in which I have excelled – be they great achievements or, seemingly, trivial ones. I can also learn to go beyond merely recalling and reliving the 'success memories' of certain facets of my life by summoning the inner courage to replicate them in the not-so-successful areas.

Like a plant that requires constant nurture, I will take it upon myself to constantly oversee the growth of my self-confidence by feeding it with information of my accomplishments on a day-to-day basis, regardless of how 'small' these accomplishments may appear to those around me. And, because I am pragmatic enough to accept that no dream or aspiration is ever fulfilled through inertia, I won't wait for golden opportunities to come my way but, instead, seize the initiative by creating my very own. Rather than being unduly concerned with my biological age in relation to timescales when it comes to the realisation of my dreams, I will view my age as an asset, and never as a liability, in my march towards finding and fulfilling my life's purpose.

I can learn to embrace the idea that exuding self-belief is a must in all that I do, or aim to accomplish in my life; believing in myself, no matter what, is pivotal to all my future successes. And whilst I appreciate that the world around me is filled with its fair share of cynics – individuals whose number one obsession is to constantly remind me of those things they feel I cannot achieve – it is what I truly believe within my soul that counts. There will also be doubters, who, from time to time, may ridicule my dreams by forming their own opinions of what they believe my limitations to be. Through it all, I am prepared to take it on the chin, simply because the world's view of me, or what I should be, is nothing in comparison to the image that stares back at me when I gaze into the mirror – an image which represents my true identity as portrayed by my core essence.

So long as I am willing to bridge the gap between positive visualisation and actualisation every one of my dream and aspirations can become a reality against all the odds. I may experience the occasional dent in my belief, courtesy of an unexpected adversity, however, my hope and optimism and the courage to persist will all remain impregnable fortresses. Even though the process of reaching my goals may not always be the most savoury there is, I remain upbeat that every time I am prepared to endure and look beyond an adversity, there will always be an opportunity for me to grow in mental strength and, more significantly, flourish in every aspect of my life.

Day 70

Every big positive change starts in small phases; whilst I may not be able to change the world, I am, in my own little way, more than capable of making my own unique and significant contribution to it.

I will dedicate today to soul-searching in the quest to discover where my strengths truly lie. For I know that within me lies an empowering force which helps me to overcome life's numerous obstacles – even the kind of adversities which have the propensity to obliterate my dreams before they have seen the light of day.

The diverse nature and variation of human talent and equality of opportunities available for every man and woman to thrive, should they be determined to do so, assures me of success irrespective of the colour of my skin, physical attributes and sexual orientation. Whether I'm black or white; African, Asian, or Caucasian; physically imposing or slight in stature; gay or straight, I know that I can excel in any area of human endeavour I genuinely set my heart and mind to. Regardless of my faith and personal philosophy – be it Christianity, Islam, Hinduism, Buddhism or atheism – or what the world makes of it, I will not be deterred from leading a life built on authenticity and making a positive contribution to society.

Day 71

As long as I genuinely feel alright and at peace within, I am more than prepared to face each of life's external challenges; be it by day or by night.

Because I know that I am more than capable of being in control of my thoughts and corresponding emotions, I believe I can attain both the right composure and frame of mind needed to detach myself from problematic situations in order to tackle them objectively.

In terms of my life's challenges and accompanying daily pressures, I believe that I am always at an advantage, for the simple reason that I am alive and blessed with the powers of both lateral and divergent thinking which are integral to the art of problem-solving. And as long as I continue to see adversity as an inanimate element which lacks that human potential of thought and reason, I will neither be out-thought, nor out-fought by it.

In any difficult situation, I can choose hope and optimism over fear and, likewise, learn to embrace courage over rumination and anxiety. No matter how despairing or despondent I feel owing to the druggy effects of yesterday's dark clouds over my bid to attain clarity, I can tune in to the shimmering rays of sunshine that today and tomorrow offers. As long as I'm willing to keep my chin up, it will be but a matter of time for the bright lights of life-enhancing splendour I have long been seeking, pierce through my soul. For the traits of the born optimist within me form the basis of my conviction that I possess that unique ability to connect with my inner powers of foresight to view clear pathways to my own personal prosperity in the midst of countless roadblocks and impediments. Whatever challenge comes my way, my confidence levels and ability to adapt and thrive, even in the harshest of life's situations will continue to rise. For I am, on a day-to-day basis, learning to inculcate into my stream of consciousness the notion that every adversity I face represents a transitional phase and never a permanent state of affairs. For the firmer my conviction that I can scale every hurdle in my lane regardless of their height, weight or magnitude, the brighter my prospects will be of finding golden opportunities within each adversity erected in my path. And so long as the obstacles in my path cannot think, breathe, plan or strategise like I can, I will always have the edge over them.

Day 72

With my sights firmly set on the imminent breakthroughs of today and tomorrow I see no further need to enslave myself to memories of yesterday's disappointments.

Because the word 'possibility' and the phrase 'fear of failure' would make strange bedfellows it is highly unlikely I'll gain any kind of mastery over the former if I continue to entertain a mindset that is subservient to the latter.

As another day dawns, I resolve to adopt brand new ways of thinking, as expecting outdated ideas to solve new problems would most definitely be an unworthy cause. And rather than dwell on, or be consumed by, the failings of my past, I can choose the self-improvement and opportunity-enhancing option of learning from such errors. Instead of being paralysed with debilitating emotions and despondent thoughts of what might have been, I can be optimistic that I am still alive and able to experience the kind of challenges that get me out of bed in the morning and makes living worthwhile.

Dedicating each moment to cleansing my life of baleful and funereal thoughts will not only feed my mind with new, revitalising elements of positivity, but also put me in a mental and physical state of preparedness to grab that once-in-a-lifetime opportunity as soon as it presents itself. I am all too aware that the word 'success' oftentimes operates like a train schedule and, in terms of its arrival and departure times, it is imperative for me to be on the right 'platform', with a mindset that is prepared and ready to board that 'success train' when it arrives.

The born optimist within has today spoken of the value of making the most of little. This inner voice of wisdom encourages me to remain awake, alert and in an anticipatory mode to seek out opportunities and, even when these opportunities aren't immediately presented to me, within me lies the resources to create and maximise them.

Day 73

In a world filled with 'icebergs' a 'Titanic' way of thinking is the last thing I need.

Dynamism is an art worth learning in terms of coping mechanisms when surfing the, often tempestuous tidal, waves of life's oceans. And, as for those niggling fears and anxieties that once sought refuge within me, I believe they have long overstayed their welcome. Hence, the time has come to replace despondency with contagious enthusiasm for my future prospects.

Whilst I am under no illusion that there will be dark clouds and storms every now and again threatening to capsize my ship of dreams before it has even begun to set sail, I cling on to that inner conviction that there is, and always will be, a ray of hope and optimism piercing through every dark cloud above my head. And as long as I choose to lift my head up to spot, and walk in the path of, that piercing light shining on me, avoiding every lurking iceberg on the route to success is a strong possibility. If I am willing to pause for a moment to review my ineffective strategies, with a view to reflecting on the fruitless nature of my old ways, I can be rest assured that positive change is but one behavioural change away. For with this change of which I speak will come a new chapter, and a new path leading to my personal success and prosperity.

As I step out of my comfort zone into the warm embrace of another glorious day, I hold on to the conviction that I am blessed with the gift of foresight to not only identify, but also avert, the huge iceberg that lies ahead, threatening to upturn my vessel of dreams, as I navigate it to the shores of reality. Whilst I know that there will be days when the pessimist within me would deem the entire world as a cold, lonely and frightening place, I am reminded that also within me somewhere is a dormant giant waiting to rise and claim its rightful place in its attainment of immeasurable success.

On some occasions I may feel negative emotions owing to the daunting task of making unilateral decisions on subjects in which I lack both the expert knowledge and experience. When that time comes, the born optimist within will, once again, spring into life and encourage me to seek out the opinion of those with a proven track record of success in those areas. For it makes perfect sense to appreciate that those who have succeeded in the areas in which I need help would be able to impart the much needed invaluable knowledge that can positively impact my journey through life. I am reminded that no man or woman is, and ever will be, an all-knowing organism; for where one individual's knowledge ceases tends to be the very point the next person's commences.

Day 74

The positive use of my thoughts is what transforms the virtual 'nothing' of my life into an actual 'something'.

My greatest possession in life isn't material – not a house, car, clothes, jewellery, financial net worth or money in the bank – but my mental resources. For I can use the resources I already possess to procure the things that I am genuinely in need of. With the judicious use of my mind I can breed positive thoughts that will go a long way in catapulting my life's goals and aspirations from the realm of obscurity to the corridors of success.

Using my thoughts positively means putting together realistic action plans that are in alignment with every vision my mind conceives on a regular basis. From writing such aspirations down, to internalising and verbalising them, until my entire state of being and future objectives in life become one. I also owe it to myself to assume the role of my life's 'success mid-wife'; that individual whose sole aim in life is to deliver each and every dream and aspiration conceived. The onus, as ever, will be on me to ensure that these goals, conceived in the refuge of my mind from birth, childhood, right through to adulthood, do not become stillborn. For my mind, and the thoughts it produces, are my most prized possession; the appropriate use of which has the potency to not only break down all manner of barriers, but also stem the flow of every tidal wave and tempest life presents to me.

If I so will it, not only can the power of my mind move every hitherto perceived insurmountable mountain, it can also help transform every little infant step I take into gigantic strides in my march towards personal prosperity.

Day 75

I may not possess all the things most men and women my age possess but within me lies the potential to achieve the things few men and women my age can only imagine, let alone achieve.

Whilst I am well aware of my capabilities, I also know that what I put into use on a day-to-day basis in terms of my ability is but a fraction of my actual potential. And whilst I am not oblivious to the fact that I still have certain areas of 'potential strength' that can be improved upon to become 'actual strength', this knowledge will only spur me on in the constant pursuit of self-improvement and the enhancement of my already identified potential and inner resources.

I can take solace in the notion that even the men and women who are proven experts in their chosen fields still strive for improvement; and the day I stop aiming to develop myself marks the beginning of the end in terms of any potential for personal growth.

On my quest for progression and self-improvement I will desist from spending my precious time and existence moping and ruminating over past setbacks and disappointments. And even when my peers seem to be flying ahead of me, I will not despair; for success, to me, is, and will continue to be, measured subjectively. From this day on, my own definition of 'success' or 'being successful' will be what I deem it to be and never be restricted to the myopic confines of society's definitions or interpretations.

I will embrace the art of being unique; in a world of like for like, differentiation will forever be instrumental to not just my survival, but also thriving as an individual. Gazing into my mental mirror, the image that is projected back to me is that of someone who is slowly, but surely, building bridges in order to connect his current situation with a much improved one.

As human beings, we may all share similar physical features and personality traits, the truth however remains that no two individuals – man, woman, or child – are entirely identical in terms of their upbringing, background and life experiences. For not only do these distinct experiences help to shape and influence the nature of my values, goals and future aspirations as a unique human being, they also help to serve as a reminder to never compare my position in life to that of others.

Surely, there ought to be more to my life than simply being put on this earth to compete with others. What if I was born to add to the contribution of others, and never to take away from it? Or what if my purpose is to – in my own little way – leave the world a better place than the one I was born into?

I have, with intense admiration, often observed the fleet of swans I see swimming along the River Great Ouse, which cuts through a place called 'Embankment' in the beautiful town of Bedford, with a view to learning all I can from these wondrous creatures of nature. Even though these birds all bear similar traits in terms of their style, grace and elegance, they all still seem to take pride in their individual uniqueness. Even though there are noticeable differences in the colour of their feathers and the patterns and directions in which they all swim, they still learn to accommodate each other's differences along the same river space. I am open to learning from these birds of beauty that hardly ever encroach upon each other's territory. And whilst they all shine in their individual splendour, collectively, they contribute immensely to this historical town's growing tourism.

It remains clear to me that every time I choose to follow the dictates of my heart, by sticking to my very own unique purpose in life, I am increasing the pool of diverse benefits waiting to be reaped by humankind through future generations yet unborn. From this day onwards, learning to embrace diversity and differentiation will remain central to how I think, what I say and, consequently, the things I do.

Day 76

The potential to rise above and beyond yesterday and today's setbacks significantly lies in my unwavering pursuit of a better tomorrow.

I know there will be moments in my life when I find myself stuck between the proverbial rock and a hard place; similarly, there will be occasions when problems come at me full-throttle but the pace of my much-needed solutions to the very same problems will be pedestrian-like. But through the eye of life's most precarious storms, I will obstinately continue to march on; safe in the knowledge that there is always a worse place to be in life. And right in the thick of such harrowing experiences will I learn to embrace a spirit of calm; consciously replacing panic with a contemplative spirit and reflective soul. I will recall my past achievements and this will serve as a source of inner motivation when searching for solutions to the challenges of today. I will also pause to reflect upon those positive spells in my life that saw me persisting on, rather than desisting from the cause, in order to achieve my desired goal, regardless of how negligible these accomplishments may seem now.

By activating my memory of how I overcame adversity, I will become more energised and empowered with the self-belief I need to transform what was once a mere hope into a concrete optimism. Likewise, the memories of the setbacks I have experienced; rather than despise them, I can learn to employ them as learning tools, techniques and strategies to avert future repetitions.

Day 77

I will not allow my mind and body to be defeated by negative pressures of any kind. The only pressure I will submit to is the empowering kind from within that allows me to pursue every one of my goals, dreams and aspirations.

Even when I am knocked of my perch a million and one times, on the way to the actualisation of my goals, I will not be fazed. And should I be tempted to capitulate to life's challenges and negative pressures, I will seek first to understand how I can transform these overwhelming forces into a launch-pad to propel me towards my desired objectives.

There will be times when my spirit will be exhausted and close to being broken in a chain of unfortunate events. There will also be times when I'll feel too ill-equipped to overcome life's difficulties heading my way at cheetah-like speed. But come those moments when life decides it has nothing better to do than to rear its ugly head, within me will rise a stronger vocal force which disputes and combats all traces of self-limiting thoughts and pessimistic beliefs. And from within will come forth an irrepressible voice that not only helps me to write my very own script of victory but also encourages me stick to the relentless pursuit of my personal calling. There will also be days when everything I aim to achieve appears to be collapsing before my very eyes, with my lifelong aspirations and visions of the future, seemingly, evaporating into thin air.

In the midst of this chaos, one thing will remain unchanged in my quest for victory: the vision of the golden horizons that lay ahead of me on my journey through life's setbacks and despairing situations. A self-reminder of where I've been and the firm knowledge of who I am, and what I can become, will be the fuel that continues to drive me, even when the self-limiting thoughts of failure threaten to debilitate me. Regardless of how extremely difficult I perceive my life's current conditions or ordeal, it is still possible to paint myself a positive mental picture of the exact kind of future I crave – a sparkling image of tomorrow borne out of the fortitude and resilience I exhibit today. From the very heart of life's carnage can still come that one opportunity which transforms my situation from uncertainty to prosperity.

Whilst there is no doubt that the foundation of my hope, optimism and courage will, every now and again, be shaken to its very core by life's adversities, being deprived from realising my goals, dreams and aspirations will be a different proposition altogether.

Day 78

Whilst the positive changes I aspire to in my life may have begun in droplets of water, they can eventually flow with the impact of an ocean.

I am prepared to accept that the changes I seek in certain areas of my life may not be automatic. I am also aware that it would not only take the right focus, determination and dedication on my part, to succeed, but also constant practice and day-to-day mental preoccupation with the very goals I aim to accomplish.

Even though I am prepared to leave the windows of my mind open to allow the entry of various external motivational influences to enable me achieve my goals, I will not do so at the expense of my own inner motivation vehicle – my bedrock for sustainable personal success. And even though the 'whats', 'whens' and 'hows' of the things I do, or set out to achieve, are important, they aren't nearly as crucial as the 'whys' behind my choosing to do or achieve those very things in the first instance.

If the 'whats, 'whens' and 'hows' serve as the drivers of my inner motivational vehicle, the 'whys' are responsible for fuelling and refuelling the engine of that inner motivation vehicle; without the 'whys', attaining any sort of successful outcomes would be an exercise in futility.

The real change I seek will not come from the outside world, but emanate from the world within. For positive change to happen in my life, it requires a genuine inward consent from me. My inner consent for change and success takes priority over outward influences or external imposition.

Not until I feel the genuine need for change deeply in my heart and mind – whilst reminding myself of my genuine motivational reason(s) behind that particular change – will the prospect of realising that change become reality. To rid my life of stagnation, I must, with an open mind, allow the benefits of change to replace what I perceive to be detrimental to its progress in my daily stream of consciousness.

Day 79

Whilst being gracious in defeat is essential for the strengthening of my character, showing magnanimity in my victories is integral to winning hearts and minds.

Although winning is important in all that I do, it isn't nearly as uplifting and personally rewarding as my acceptance of the idea that setbacks will always be a part of my life, alongside its successes. Not to mention how learning to examine the impact of my past failings would be by far nobler than seeking to defend or justify them.

I can learn from the men and women who have succeeded me, the very important philosophy that what makes the experience of victory in my life priceless, is sometimes being on the receiving end of defeat.

I will also seek to avert the perception of defeat as an end in itself; and instead choose to view every defeat as the type of adversity that can potentially present me with opportunities to learn, grow, improve and give that venture another go.

And in all that I do, the spirit of equanimity will remain an integral aspect of my life. For it is the glue that holds everything else in my life together: from my mental composure to my behavioural consistency and rules for living which manifests itself in all my interpersonal relationships. Similarly, the prospect of maintaining a calm temperament in the face of the most challenging of trials is most definitely a virtue worthy of applause. And like all things that are truly worth having, learning to adopt a serene temperament through the sunshine of victory or the rainclouds of defeat will not only bring down multi-

186

tudes of barriers in my path to success and self-actualisation, it will also ensure I remain the author of my own destiny as against being fate's victim or plaything.

As I this morning embrace a brand new era, I will do well to remember that successful living for me could, perhaps, mean taking the good with the bad and finding the middle ground for moderation. I may not be able to have complete control over all of my life's outcomes, be they desirable or unsavoury, but if there remains one element of my life I can gain mastery over, it is to choose the right attitude and reaction in every situation in which I find myself. For in any given set of circumstances, I believe that I have an exclusive right to my choice of response and demeanour.

Being magnanimous in victory can be matched with humility in defeat – I must be prepared to embrace correction and feedback; especially when the suggestion of change comes from others rather than me. Long gone are the days when I blindly believed that no one else has the right or authority to highlight my shortcomings; especially when the intent is constructive and aimed at improving me as a person.

Although the road to true greatness does begin from constructive self-appraisal, without being unduly self-critical, I can also learn to instil within me the notion that genuine happiness and success will continue to be an illusory concept if I refuse to acknowledge that seeking the counsel of those who excel in the areas in which I struggle is nothing to be ashamed of. And rather than viewing the art of tapping into such an individual's reservoir of knowledge as weakness, I could, instead, treat it as a pathway to true greatness.

Treading the noble path of humility for me would mean being honest with myself and others when the occasion demands to acknowledge errors – both past and present – and to be penitent enough to do the appropriate 'U-turns' in areas where I've fallen short of the required standards.

With a new day comes fresh resolve to be at peace with the setbacks of yesterday; with the humility to seek advice from those who have been through similar trials and have overcome them. And with a renewed sense of hope, optimism and the courage to pursue my dreams, I will stare straight ahead into the horizon of success with a day by day action plan to guide me through each step of the way.

Setbacks and disappointments are, and will continue to be, what I am willing to perceive them to be – either as that final destination where everything else grinds to a halt or, perhaps, more favourably, a 'pit stop' where I am merely stopping to reflect, refuel and push forward. If my ultimate aim is to prosper in all that I do, can there really be any sense in wasting precious time ruminating and stagnating when I could, instead, channel my energy towards attaining my goals?

Day 80

I have no need to fear or despair; for it is my hope, optimism and the courage to achieve the seemingly impossible that got me here.

Today is the day my journey, which begun at the point of hope, transiting through optimism, finally arrives at the gateway of courage. Due to the sometimes complex web of life's obstacles that I have encountered and have, in the past, had to untangle myself from, I remain stronger than ever; rooted, unmoved and enthusiastic about the challenges which lay ahead. And rather than seeking to avoid difficulties by exercising the so-called 'safety behaviours' in relation to these hardships, I will, with open arms, embrace future adversities for what I am able to learn from them.

Today marks the turning point in my perception of challenges and obstacles; for what I once perceived as 'failure' on my part would now be nothing more than a setback from which my re-invigorated life – through my renewed positive outlook and attitude – can stage a series of bounce-backs. Fuelled and powered by the 'whys' behind the goals and objectives I continue to set myself, my inner motivation vehicle will transport me from where I am today to where I aspire to be tomorrow. With this final day on my journey comes the understanding that my 'whys' are the adversity-proof elements that help to transform a once vulnerable and half-hearted motivation within me into its juggernaut-like counterpart. And in the style of a true juggernaut, obstacles may sometimes slow down my personal drive; derailing it, however, is a different story altogether. Likewise, adversity and life's numerous challenges may suppress my inner motivation occasionally, but will never succeed in bringing

189

it to a complete halt. And whilst this juggernaut-like inner motivation of mine will be subject to delay from time to time, it will never be denied in its ultimate quest to fulfil its life's purpose.

Like the next man or woman, I have my own actual strengths and potential strengths – the former being my established assets and the latter representing areas that can be improved. I, and I alone, possess the potential to strengthen and increase my assets to a significant level in order to overcome each of life's hurdles that stand between me and success.

There will be no more sleepless nights and restlessness, or leading a life driven by fear – I will, instead, follow a path motivated by visions of possibilities; for the time has come when a daily celebration of my own inner strengths and accomplishments will be my mantra.

I will not be deluded by trivialising the gravity of the task that lies before me and neither will I be under any illusion that the acquisition of hope and optimism automatically entitles me to success..

I am aware that my ability to successfully invoke the spirit of the born optimist within me will, occasionally, be as a consequence of endless diligence, dedication and mental introspection built over time. And this quality can only be nurtured by learning to strike a near perfect balance between self-love and altruism. Furthermore, I will strive for enlightenment in all that I do – particularly in areas where I find potential, rather than actual, strength.

Above all, I will try to remember that the acquisition of knowledge in itself means nothing. Whilst my insatiable thirst to attain, and replenish, my knowledge may mean something, it is how I employ the knowledge I've acquired, to improve self and enhance quality of other people's lives, that means everything.

Motivational Philosophies from the Mind of the Author

1.   It's not the thought of who we are that drives us to leave the comfort of our bed each morning, but the thought of who we choose to be or refuse to become.

2.   The true worth of any knowledge, power, or influence we possess in any area of our lives, at any point in time, lies solely in our ability to use such gifts to replenish, and never diminish, the lives of others.

3.   Constant sleep and slumbering equals constant slothfulness. A society that constantly sleeps and slumbers is bound to become poverty's favourite playground.

4.   In a world littered with wrong choices and ill-advised decisions let us embrace knowledge and enlightenment as our trusted companions; for they are to the human mind what a compass is to a lost sailor at sea.

5.   Negative public opinion should not derail any man, woman or child's dedication to the pursuit of their goals; for it is what we passionately believe in within our hearts and minds that will influence the work of our hands.

6.   In any kingdom where dishonesty, falsity and deception makes up its subjects, truth is the king and will forever rule; for it always prevails.

7.   Humankind can peacefully navigate its way through life's murky waters if we all adopt an open-minded 'we' way of thinking instead of a parochial-minded 'I' or 'me' mindset. We can create a world where 'collaboration' prevails over 'domination' or 'isolation' ; and rather than perceive 'interdependency' as weakness, embrace it as a symptom of true greatness.

8.   We owe it to ourselves and no one else to rule our own minds. For an uncontrolled mind is no different to an aircraft's autopilot system; whilst it has been developed to fly unaided, it still requires human monitoring to avert a crash.

9.   Knowledge in itself is nothing; and whilst striving to acquire it may stand for something, applying that knowledge for the purpose of self-improvement and the common good means everything.

10.   The most impactful form of human motivation isn't that which is externally-imposed upon us, or derived from others, but that that which we are able to generate from within ourselves.

11.   A mind that fails to think laterally is a mind that sinks perpetually into the vast abyss of emptiness. The effective use of our minds is our most powerful resource; we can use the things we have at our mental disposal today to procure the things we need tomorrow.

12.   The more we remind ourselves of the mountains of adversity we've successfully climbed in our lives, the stronger we are in coping with the pebbles of problems that litter our feet today.

13. We are all 'artists', responsible for painting the pictures of our own destinies. Similarly, we are 'captains' responsible for navigating our 'ship of dreams' to the shores of reality.

14. The minute hope and optimism for the future evaporates, our potential, ability and the courage to survive adversity, let alone excel in anything, begins to disintegrate.

15. 'Authenticity' should always take precedence over 'popularity' – for the things we do in accordance with the dictates of our hearts, conscience and our personal values, override those that are done merely for external applause.

16. It is perhaps better to live a life devoid of dreams than one congested with dreams but devoid of the will and passion to pursue those very dreams.

17. It is perhaps better to try and fail in any venture or undertaking, than live the rest of our lives knowing we failed to try.

18. Whilst the person we are, and the person we've been, are, to a vast degree, influenced by the nature of our upbringing, enduring life lessons, environment, social orientation and associations; the person we can become will solely be determined by our inner decisions.

19. We can grow from being mere anticipators to real initiators of positive change.

20.   We cannot enlighten ignorance by ignoring the path leading to enlightenment.

Author's life journey

Jamal Lanre Shashore was born and raised in Lagos, Nigeria. His father was a journalist and his mother, a film editor in television broadcasting. Coming from, what many would consider, a privileged background, Jamal's early childhood was happy and a bright future, seemingly, lay ahead of him. However, the breakdown of his parents' marriage led to a long period of instability, uncertainty and personal hardship. In the year 2000, Jamal relocated to the United Kingdom, in search of new purpose and meaning in his life.

Almost two decades later, having experienced redundancy, impoverishment and even homelessness along the way, Jamal has successfully transformed his own personal adversities into triumph and achievement by authoring two life-enhancing books, with *Ten Statements: The 10 Success Recipes for Romantic Relationships* being his debut publication in 2009 (under the pen name of 'JL Shash').

More recently, he launched the Born Motivated Training Project; a self-motivation training and education initiative aimed at empowering people of diverse backgrounds and circumstances with the mental discipline, life skills and techniques to overcome personal struggles and achieve success.

Jamal and his family currently live in Bedfordshire, in the UK.

Closing Acknowledgements

My heartfelt appreciation goes to the following people - in no particular order, of course - for the positive value you have all brought (and continue to bring) to my life in your own unique ways:

Okomayin family (Lewis, Yetunde, Elsie and Hayley), Mark Kelly, Ildi Bokor, Jani Bokor, Ben Spence, Michael Akanji, Andrew Parker, Bobby Ayorinde, Obafemi Okusanya, Adefemi Sosanya, Chief Bolaji Ayorinde, Chief Mrs C.A Ayorinde, Mrs Margaret Okusanya, Ivana Polakova, Emma Coombs, Adegboyega Ajayi, Marie Bedding, Andy Lewington, Duncan McMillan, Dapo Otubanjo, Janet Riley, Kallee and Michael Bradford, Dean Venn, Andy Leeks, Dean Sykes, Matt 'Super Guitarist' Turnbull, Chidi Dennar, Dipo Ogundipe, Adedayo Oso, Adewunmi Yusuf, Seyi Eniayewu, Mobolade Ayorinde, Mrs Bolanle Adesina, Mrs Oyebola Aduroja, Jude Nebamor, Mrs Yemi Adeyemi, Mrs Adeola Filani, Winston Amole, Adesola Kadri, The Odeniyi family (including Eniola and Laolu), Ibukunoluwa Mamora, Yusuf Fuhad, Abiola and Tolu Kadri, Jade Simmonds, Rachel Ajose, and not forgetting the entire members of Team Ben at Lifesearch.

My eternal indebtedness and special gratitude also goes to:

Mrs Ajani, my primary school English Language teacher who instilled in me a sense of self-belief that I can achieve anything I genuinely set my heart and mind to. And Mr Joshua Omoruyi Obadagbonyi; not only were you the most amazing 'dad' to me growing up, you were also the best mentor I could ever have wished for. May both your gentle souls rest in eternal peace.

L - #0147 - 130519 - C0 - 210/148/11 - PB - DID2515118